BEACON HILL

BEACON HILL

The Life & Times of a Neighborhood

MOYING LI-MARCUS

Northeastern Univesity Press

Boston

NORTHEASTERN UNIVERSITY PRESS

LIBRARY OF CONGRESS CATALOGING-IN PUBLICATION DATA
Li-Marcus, Moying, 1954–
Beacon Hill : the life and times of a neighborhood / Moying Li-Marcus.
p.   cm.
Includes bibliographical references and index.
ISBN 1-55553-543-7 (alk. paper)
1. Beacon Hill (Boston, Mass.)—History. 2. Boston (Mass.)—History. I. Title.
F73.68.B4 L5 2002
974.4'61—dc21   2002008213

Book design and typography in Adobe Jenson by Christopher Kuntze.
Printed and bound by Thomson-Shore, Inc., Dexter, Michigan.
The paper is Fortune Matte, an acid-free stock.

FRONTISPIECE: Courtesy of Helen Eddy

MANUFACTURED IN THE UNITED STATES OF AMERICA
06   05   04   03   02   5   4   3   2   1

FOR *Paul*

CONTENTS

Noisy, silent, crooked, straight, lights out early, lights on late,
Boston's high hat, low brow meets, on Beacon Hill, in little streets.

MINA DEHART MIDDLETON

ACKNOWLEDGMENTS

To acknowledge all the people who have helped me with this book is to express my indebtedness and gratitude to those who have shared my curiosities as well as the uncertainties that come with this kind of search for answers. Several fellow residents and members of the Civic Association, Chris Pratt and Peter Thomson in particular, have given me their unconditional support from the inception of the project, despite the capricious nature of the journey. To my friends and former professors, David Hall of Harvard University and Alan Lawson of Boston College, I owe a deep debt for their unfailing support and careful reading of the manuscript. I am also grateful to Professor Thomas O'Connor of Boston College for his guidance and encouragement. I owe a special debt of gratitude to my longtime friend and editor, Richard Harley of World Development Productions, a prize-winning author and filmmaker, who guided the manuscript through its final revisions.

My appreciation also goes to Alexandra Marshall, Sandy Steele, and Suzanne Besser of Beacon Hill, to my friends Debbie Kee, Steve Andress, Philip Greenspun, David Scudder, and to my mother-in-law, Kay Pease. I also want to thank members of the historic research committee that was formed to assist me with research for the project: Mary Thomsen, Mary Pat Cleary, Gail Weesner, Bernard Borman, Paul Greenfield, Nancy Leslie, Anastasia Kucharsky, Linda Cox, Kathy Stern, and Tom Clemens.

I am indebted to John Cronin, Chief Librarian of the *Boston Herald*, to Aaron Schmidt of the Print Department of the Boston Public Library, to Nancy Richard of the Bostonian Society, to Frances O'Donnell of the Andover-Harvard Theological Library, to Greg Perkins of the Boston Redevelopment Authority, and to Lorna Condon of the Society for the Preservation of New England Antiquities for their patience and assistance with my research. I am grateful to all fellow Beacon Hillers who have generously lent me their autobiographies, family letters, and photos, not to mention their valuable memories. To Beacon Hill Civic Association, I would like to express my gratitude for its support of the project as well as its seminal contribution to the historical development of one of the oldest neighborhoods in America. I also wish to extend my appreciation to Bill Frohlich, Ann Twombly, and Jill Bahcall of Northeastern University Press for their expertise and generous support in the publication of this book. My deepest gratitude goes to my husband, Paul, whose family first settled in Boston in 1634. Without his unfailing encouragement, faith, and good humor, this book would not have been possible.

In the end, this is very much a continuation of a journey I embarked on more than twenty years ago, except that the questions I ask now are more concrete, and the people I come into contact with have become my friends and neighbors.

PREFACE

My passage to Beacon Hill began in the late 1970s with a journey to America—from China. I had been studying at Beijing Foreign Studies University when an American professor approached me with an offer to further my education in the United States. At the time I had a rather confused vision of that remote place across the sea. For decades, the "land of the free" came across in our official media as a kind of "evil empire." It was not until Secretary of State Henry Kissinger began his clandestine meetings with Premier Zhou En Lai in the 1970s that positive publicity about the United States started to emerge. The normalization of relations between the two countries in 1979 signaled, for me, a green light to go West. Armed with a generous scholarship and a plane ticket from Swarthmore College, I left China on August 6, 1980, for Philadelphia, the "city of brotherly love."

But who were these Americans, I wondered. What forces had made them who they were—and what they aspired to be? The search for answers launched me on a journey that would prove much longer than I could have imagined, including graduate studies in American history. But it wasn't until I encountered a place called Beacon Hill in Boston that I began to see America from a deeper, more personal perspective. It was in Beacon Hill, one of the oldest neighborhoods in the nation, where my husband and I found the house we both love and came to call home. Walking through the streets of Beacon Hill, getting to know the neighbors day by day, I felt my questions surfacing once more: How many of the popular stories and myths of Beacon Hill were well-founded? How much had been a later embellishment? How important in the formative years were links with the peoples and markets of remote lands like China? And why has this particular neighborhood continued to grow, preserving so many of its historic buildings and traditions, when relatively little has survived in other American communities that date back to the early years?

The opportunity to explore Beacon Hill's story emerged on Christmas Eve of 1996 when Tanya Holton, then the Executive Director of the Beacon

Hill Civic Association, asked if I would be interested in writing a contemporary historical account for the seventy-fifth anniversary of the Association. In the past books had been written on the early history of Beacon Hill, she said, but few of these books have bridged the past with the present. This was the beginning of a commitment that took me onto a rather unpredictable path, which, in retrospect, is the biggest gift this neighborhood has given me.

Following the streets of Beacon Hill, looking behind the redbrick walls that whisper stories of bygone eras, and chatting with old-timers who've called this place home all their lives, I found myself engaged in an intimate dialogue, sharing the laughter and sorrows of this special place, its victories and failures, its foibles and grandeur, its complexities and, sometimes, confusions. Here on Beacon Hill, history has come to life for me.

After several years of such "intimate dialogues" with the neighborhood, I have come to the realization that if there is a myth about Beacon Hill, it is that the Hill's residents, generation after generation, continue to create their own history. Indeed, Beacon Hill's history might be seen as "myths in the making"—a dynamic process for over three hundred years, whereby Beacon Hillers have never ceased to write their own stories while integrating the past into plans for the future. With each generation, Beacon Hill is reinvented.

The people of Beacon Hill have encouraged me along my journey, and many have become companions in this search for answers. My hope is that "the old" and "the new" of Beacon Hill, seen in a fresh, personal light, will not just benefit those of us who live on the Hill, but also help others to have a glimpse of a piece of Americana.

CHAPTER ONE

A New Vision for an Old Hill

1630–1900

There have been books on the slope of Beacon Hill
when the wolves still howled on the summit.

VAN WYCK BROOKS
The Flowering of New England

THE SHAWMUT PENINSULA

WILLIAM BLACKSTONE liked the Shawmut peninsula because it was a place where he could finally be alone with his books. Or so he thought. He had first laid eyes on the peninsula in 1623 as a member of British Captain Robert Gorges's expedition to settle the Massachusetts Bay area. At twenty-seven, Blackstone (or Blaxton) had signed up as assistant pastor to the expedition, freshly ordained out of Emmanuel College, Cambridge. Unfortunately, the colonization he hoped to promote soon went awry, and most of the settlers hightailed it back to England after only a year.

William Blackstone, however, was not on board. He, for one, found the peninsula a most congenial place. Shawmut, an Indian name meaning living fountains, seemed very safe to Blackstone. It was virtually defended by its own geography, surrounded by water on all sides but one, with only a narrow neck or causeway linking peninsula to mainland. At high tide, the peninsula became an island. Shawmut's hills peaked at about 150 feet, forming what would later be called Beacon Hill or Sentry Hill. There any incoming and outgoing traffic could easily be seen. West of Beacon, toward the Charles River, was Mount Vernon. To the east was Pemberton Hill, or Cotton Hill, names that would later all be subsumed by "Beacon Hill." The south side of the hills was specially blessed with gentle sea breezes and full exposure to the sun. Here the pastor rejoiced to discover springs of sweet water. Shawmut was, for him, the perfect place to call home. Here he would put down roots and start to enjoy his own company amid a library of two hundred books imported from the motherland.

Blackstone's coveted solitude was short-lived. By the spring of 1630, a new group of colonists was heading his way—an eleven-ship fleet launched out of England. Many on board were leading Puritans of the day, ready to start an experimental community in the newly chartered Massachusetts Bay Colony. On the high seas, aboard the flagship *Arbella*, the new governor, John Winthrop, tried to articulate his sense of the moment in a prophetic sermon. "We shall be as a City upon a Hill," he announced. "The eyes of all people are upon us."[1] The sense of biblical destiny was conscious and deliberate. After braving the stormy Atlantic for more than three months, with few naviga-

OPPOSITE:
Beacon Hill, chromolithograph by J. H. Bufford, from an 1811 watercolor by J. R. Smith. Courtesy of the Boston Public Library. The Beacon on Beacon Hill has gone through several transformations. First built in 1634, the Beacon was blown down in 1789. It was replaced by a brick monument topped with a gilded eagle, as viewed here, in 1790 at the corner of Derne and Temple Streets. Soon it was torn down again to make room for the expansion of the State House.

tional aids, the travelers found a place for their new home—the hill without a city, and a population of one lonesome expatriate pastor.

Actually, Winthrop and his colonists had no intention, at first, of disturbing Blackstone or his paradise. Their original destination, Salem Plantation, where they had dispatched an advance team the year before, faltered through its first long New England winter. Charlestown, where they turned next, had inadequate water supplies. When news of the colonists' plight reached him, Blackstone's Christian charity overcame his preference for solitude. He extended an invitation to the colonists to come share the sweet spring and other natural resources that had been his alone. Governor Winthrop gladly accepted the invitation, bringing with him a hundred friends who, after the initial party, decided to move in. Before long, there came more settlers. And more. By 1633 the "guests" had taken over the entire peninsula, graciously assigning the Reverend some fifty acres of what he originally thought was his own land. After only a year, Blackstone's neighbors proved too much for him altogether. He sold his land back to the town for thirty pounds, explaining that originally he had left England because of his dislike for the "Lord Bishops." Now, he said, he was losing his liking for his Puritan "Lord Brethren." Blackstone packed up for good and left Shawmut for quieter pastures in Rhode Island.

The new citizens of Shawmut, for their part, wasted no time hunkering down for the long haul. They broke ground, built, fenced, and planted. They had "all things to do," wrote Winthrop, "as in the beginning of the world."[2] They also renamed the peninsula "Boston" after the hometown of many of the settlers from Lincolnshire, England.

Sentry or Beacon Hill, courtesy of the Bostonian Society/Old State House. Tri-mountain or Beacon Hill is viewed from Charlestown.

The Reverend Blackstone's house. Courtesy of the Bostonian Society/Old State House.

A growing population brought the need for regulation. A town government soon evolved in Boston, operating through town meetings and selectmen. The town arbitrated who was given land and how much. When the flow of springwater could not meet the rising demand, the town organized the digging of new wells. The town also saw to it that individual landowners upheld their responsibility to maintain communal fences. Fines were levied on offenders. The town even decided how many cows and sheep a household should have, and where and how the cows should be herded and fed, given the limitations of pastureland on the peninsula.

The running of the town meetings and government in Boston was far from democratic during the days of Winthrop. By convention, the freemen

Overlooking the Boston Common from Beacon Hill, c.1790. Courtesy of the Boston Public Library.

who were granted the right to voice opinions and vote for selectmen were male inhabitants who had taken an oath to the Bay Colony. Social stratification was strongly influenced by the degree of wealth one could claim back in the old country. Wealth led to firmer control of power, on the one hand, and a loosening of wallets on the other. Contributions to community undertakings, such as the upkeep of free schools, were proportional to the wealth claimed. In 1636, of the 124 office and committee positions in the town, 109 were occupied by the "richer inhabitants."[3]

Under the new government, the town developed and its population steadily grew. After the first year of settlement, about two hundred people lived on the peninsula; by 1635 the number had climbed to about six hundred. These new inhabitants, in a short period of time, transformed the physical appearance of the peninsula by fencing pastureland and building new houses on its periphery. The hills, however, were left largely unchanged. Between the time Winthrop first received Blackstone's invitation in 1630 and the end of the American Revolution, Shawmut remained predominantly a pasture for cows, horses, and sheep. Pasturelands were drawn and redrawn. Fences were erected and torn down. Land was bought and sold, or passed in and out of various families. Little attempt was made in that century and a half to develop systematic plans for housing, though sporadic dwellings could be spotted on the South Slope, amid sprawling orchards and patches of wild blueberries.

WHEN PATRIOTS GATHERED

*I*N THE mid-1700s Beacon Hill still had the look of unspoiled country, covered with trees, shrubs, and wildflowers. Only a few houses dotted the area. Three were owned by John Singleton Copley, the self-taught portrait artist. Copley lived in one or all of them until his departure for England shortly before the War of Independence. A watercolor by one of his amateur contemporaries, Christian Remick, shows three Copley houses on what is today's Beacon Street, just west of the imposing mansion where Governor John Hancock lived.

The "Hancock Manor" was built in 1737 by Thomas Hancock, an uncle of John who later willed the property to his politically astute nephew. In its time the Manor was considered the finest house in all of Massachusetts Bay Colony. The three-story mansion, built in stone, overlooked the pastureland of Boston Common. The house itself was surrounded by a family estate that extended all the way from today's Joy Street on the west to Park Street on the east and from Beacon Street on the south to near Derne Street on the north.

In 1795, two years after John Hancock died, the town of Boston bought most of his family estate for four thousand pounds, designating it the site of the state's future capitol. Seven decades later, during the Civil War, the Massachusetts House of Representatives voted to demolish the once-imposing mansion, making room for expansion of the State House. The only indication of the mansion's earlier existence is an eighteen-by-twenty-one-inch bronze plaque on the capitol building wall, a rather sad reminder of a once-glorious past.

Purchase of the Hancock pastureland opened the way for development of

what became some of the choicest real estate in all of Boston, as well as construction of the Commonwealth's State House. The legislature had appointed a committee to consider a more convenient place for holding the General Court. But it was not a foregone conclusion that Boston, let alone Beacon Hill, should be that "convenient place." Other cities vied for the honor, including Worcester and Plymouth. In 1787 a precocious twenty-four-year-old architect named Charles Bulfinch submitted a bold design in favor of Boston's Beacon Hill, a plan that finally passed the legislature after eight years of deliberation.

Bulfinch's Bostonian pedigree, as well as his rising reputation as an architect, helped to sway Massachusetts lawmakers. He had grown up in Boston and graduated from Harvard College. After graduation, he drew on his family inheritance to visit architectural landmarks in France, Italy, and England. In London he became infatuated with Georgian architecture, the symmetrical, neoclassic style whose features he incorporated again and again into his American creations.

As Bulfinch patiently awaited approval of his proposal from the Massachusetts legislature, he decided to take on a new job designing the State House in neighboring Connecticut.[4] Apparently it was a tour de force, as statehouses go. Acclaim of the Connecticut project reached Massachusetts, and the legislature finally gave the go-ahead for construction of its own State House on Beacon Hill in 1795. On July 4 of that year, the cornerstone of the new State House was solemnly placed on a carriage drawn by fifteen white horses, representing the fifteen states of the Union. Once atop Beacon Hill, the cornerstone was laid by the governor and patriot Sam Adams. Standing at his side was Paul Revere, who brought not only the air of legend, but also a promise to devote his skills as a silversmith to adorn the building's dome with a copper cladding.

Whether by fate or design, the construction of the State House on Beacon Hill brought into realization, both physically and politically, the vision John Winthrop had articulated some 165 years before. The place where the Puritans first settled had, in fact, become a "city upon a hill" for all to see. In 1790, the city replaced the old harbor beacon with an elegant column, designed and erected by Bulfinch and located just behind what would soon become the official seat of state government.

OPPOSITE:

Hancock Manor, c. 1860. Courtesy of the Boston Public Library. Considered the finest house of its day, the building was constructed in 1737 and was torn down in 1863 to make way for the expansion of the State House.

THE MOUNT VERNON PROPRIETORS

*T*HE CONSTRUCTION of the State House on Shawmut became the catalyst for a fifty-year boom in real estate development, led by properties on the South Slope of Beacon Hill. On August 3, 1796, an explosive little advertisement appeared in the *Columbian Centinel:*

Harrison Gray Otis (1765–1848), painting by Gilbert Stuart, 1809. Courtesy of the Society for the Preservation of New England Antiquities.

The public are invited to turn their attention to these lands, which afford the best situations in town. . . . the varied fall of these lands is adapted to the circumstances of those who wish merely for genteel and airy situations, and of those who would unite to their advantages the convenience of boarding houses, and accommodations for business. Their proximity to the new State House renders it convenient for those who are desirous of accommodating the Members of the General Court.

It was a new vision for Beacon Hill, a vision to transform Shawmut from town to metropolis. Those who conceived the advertisement were members of an investment syndicate that came to be known as the "Mount Vernon Proprietors." The five originators were Jonathan Mason, Jr., Harrison Gray Otis, Charles Bulfinch, Joseph Woodword, and William Scollay.[5] All were persons of distinction.

Jonathan Mason, Jr., a graduate of Princeton, was a prominent lawyer and served in both the United States Senate and House. As one of the two largest shareholders among the Proprietors, Mason lived to see much of his investment come to fruition before passing away at the age of seventy-five in 1831.

The other largest shareholder was Harrison Gray Otis. After graduating from Harvard at age eighteen, Otis practiced law, then served as United States District Attorney and in 1829 as the third mayor of Boston.[6] Otis lived to the age of eighty-three, long enough to build and enjoy three mansions on Beacon Hill.

Charles Bulfinch, perhaps by virtue of his architectural reputation, also joined the Mount Vernon Proprietors. Among his Beacon Hill creations was the three-story brick house he designed for a relative in 1792, one of the oldest houses still standing on the North Slope, between Temple and Bowdoin Streets. Soon there followed another mansion between Cambridge and Lynde Streets,[7] the first of three Harrison Gray Otis houses.

A few years later, Hepzibah Swan also bought into the syndicate. Much of her wealth had come as a gift from a friend of her father. Her husband, Colonel James Swan, had a reputation for fighting bravely against the British at Bunker Hill. He spent much of his time in France, however, making and

Charles Bulfinch (1763–1844), painting by Mather Brown. Courtesy of the Harvard University Portrait Collection, gift of Francis V. Bulfinch, 1933. Copyright President and Fellows of Harvard College.

losing their collective fortunes. In 1815, on the verge of returning to Boston, Colonel Swan was arrested for indebtedness and sent to Saint-Pélagie prison, where he remained for fifteen years.[8] Shortly after his release, he passed away. In the meantime, Hepzibah Swan was raising their three daughters and managing family interests in Boston—including dealings on Beacon Hill.

The formation of the Mount Vernon Proprietors could not have been better timed. In the post-Revolutionary period, Boston's economy began to flourish, fanned by the maritime success of Yankee clippers. The Boston-based fleet shipped New England codfish, agricultural produce, and fur to the West Indies in exchange for molasses and cocoa, and eventually created shipping aisles down the coast of South America, through the Strait of Magellan, extending all the way across the Pacific in search of the famed silk and tea of China. With Boston's new prosperity, there also came a rise in population. Records show a population of eighteen thousand in Boston right after the War of Independence; by 1810 it had grown to thirty thousand, almost doubling in just two decades.

This burgeoning population would need housing. And the Mount Vernon Proprietors saw their opportunity, placing their fateful advertisement offering land to the public. Their offerings comprised some forty acres on the South Slope of Beacon Hill. The area stretched from the Charles River on the west to the original site of the State House on the east, and from Beacon Street on the south to approximately today's Pinckney Street on the north. The portrait artist Copley provided half of this land, for which he was paid fourteen thousand dollars.[9] Living in London ever since the American Revolution, Copley directed the sale from a distance through agents. Before the transaction was consummated, however, Copley changed his mind, believing that his agent was selling the property for less than its value. He would never have parted with that land, he claimed, if he had been in Boston. After much frustration and negotiation on both sides, including the involvement of Boston courts, Copley sent to Boston his son, John Singleton Copley, Jr., an English lawyer who later became Baron Lyndhurst, Lord Chancellor. Judging that the Mount Vernon Proprietors had not dealt with the issue so badly after all, the future lord chancellor settled in favor of the original agreement.

With land secured, the Mount Vernon Proprietors began in 1796 to draw up their street plans. The Proprietors believed that if persons of means (like themselves) set an example of buying and building responsibly, they would influence the quality of land development well into the future. The architect Charles Bulfinch again played the role of mastermind in the street layouts, though he worked with the land surveyor Mather Withington. Bulfinch, in traditional European style, preferred mansion houses with ample room for gardens and stables. Withington's vision for the layout was more modest. The result was a compromise. The majority of the now famous streets on the South Slope were laid out between 1799 and 1803.[10]

Most of the Proprietors purchased adjacent properties on today's Mount Vernon Street, their families remaining neighbors for generations to come. The Proprietors reached an important "gentlemen's agreement" in 1801, by which they set aside a thirty-foot lawn between the buildings and the street, with an understanding that nothing would be built on it. The agreement carried such weight that even by the late 1800s, when a new building was proposed, the neighbors spontaneously rejected it, preserving the original 1801 agreement.[11]

MOVING MOUNTAINS—LITERALLY

*I*N THEIR efforts to carve out space for public housing, the Proprietors did some rather radical surgery. In 1803 they decided to cut off the crest of Mount Vernon. A great deal of ingenuity was required to take sixty feet off the top of the massive hill, and the engineering feat created significant local excitement. In 1805 a short railroad, believed to be the first of its kind in America, was installed between the top of the hill and the Charles River in order to transport gravel and dirt. The days of iron and steel as popular construction materials were still a half century away, and the Beacon Hill railroad was made of timber and plank, appropriately tied together. Two sets of carts were fastened to a large pulley at the top of the hill. While one went up, the other went down, and men with handcarts ran up and down the hill alongside the vehicles. Gravel and dirt carted down from the top of the hill were used as material for landfill in what later became Charles Street. The operation was one of the most ambitious undertakings of its day. Harrison Gray Otis claimed that the Beacon Hill project "excited as much attention as Bonaparte's road over the Alps."[12]

After two years, Mount Vernon Hill finally came down to its current level. The Proprietors, meanwhile, wasted no time planning and building their

own mansions. Fifteen were built between 1806 and 1812 on what was the old Copley land. One of the first Bulfinch "classics" had been built for Otis in 1802 on Mount Vernon Street; by 1806 Bulfinch had erected another one for Otis on Beacon Street. A house had also been built for Jonathan Mason, Jr., in 1801 on Mount Vernon Street.[13]

Soon after, the building boom on Beacon Hill suffered a temporary setback. Political tensions once again were mounting between the young American Republic and old England, with maritime rights and other issues coming to the forefront. Jefferson's embargoes of 1807 and 1808, as well as the outbreak of war between the two countries in 1812, brought down many Bostonian fortunes built on foreign commerce. As economic depression set in, a number of those who had invested in Beacon Hill real estate were forced to sell at a loss.

Sleigh at the Otis House, 45 Beacon Street. Photograph by T. E. Marr. Courtesy of the Society for the Preservation of New England Antiquities.

Jonathan Mason House, c. 1830, lithograph by Pendleton's Lithography. Courtesy of the Boston Public Library. Built by Charles Bulfinch on Mount Vernon Street, the building was torn down in 1837.

ENCLAVE OF CHARM: LOUISBURG SQUARE

FORTUNATELY for the Hill, the economy turned upward by the late 1820s, as did interest in neighborhood development. Most notable among the later additions was the creation of Louisburg Square, destined to charm visitors for generations to come. A visitor from western Massachusetts called Louisburg Square "the one unspoiled, undefiled section of Boston which has withstood the march of progress and still clings to its age-old quaintness and charm."[14] An observer from China found that "the tranquil air there never tried to hurry me on. This brought me a refreshing stillness of mind from the midst of the life of a modern city."[15]

The Mount Vernon Proprietors began to lay out plans for Louisburg Square as early as 1826, though the area was not completed until the early 1840s. John Clark, the president of Equitable Safety Marine & Fire Insurance Company, built the first house on the square, now Number 19. The vision of a tree-lined garden square, originated by Charles Bulfinch, never left the mind of the Proprietors. In the spirit of Bulfinch, the Proprietors designed the center of the square with open space, and decided that it would remain that way forever. Caught in the spirit of proprietorship, the new resident owners gathered in the summer of 1844 at the house of John Clark, forming one of the first neighborhood civic groups in America, the Louisburg Square Proprietors' Committee.

The committee developed a simple but effective set of democratic procedures, with committee meetings called through written notice by three proprietors, and decisions made by a majority vote. One of the first rulings was to enlarge the center by eight square feet and fence it in with iron railings. Grass and trees were then planted and a fountain, which no longer exists, was built in the center. Two finishing touches added particular charm. One was

Louisburg Square from Mount Vernon Street. Courtesy of the Bostonian Society/ Old State House.

a marble statue of Aristides the Just at one end of the square, a gift from Joseph Iasigi, a new resident who was a successful merchant and the Turkish consul. At the opposite end of the square was a marble statue of Columbus, shipped from Italy in 1850.

It remains a mystery why the name Louisburg was chosen for the square. In one tradition, the name commemorates the capture of Louisburg of Cape Breton, Canada, in 1745 by a New England militia led by William Pepperrell. It is not obvious, however, how a battle from the 1700s could have had a bearing on the founding of the square. Nor is it clear why a celebrated locale in the center of a town named by settlers from Boston, England, should acquire a French name, via Canada. Was it because New Englanders fought and fell during those campaigns? Or because a direct descendant of Beacon Hill's first resident, William Blackstone, was also believed to have fallen at the Battle of Louisburg, making the two distant locations somewhat relevant to one another? We may never know.

What we do know today is that many renowned residents have graced the square over the years. Louisa May Alcott moved to Number 10 after the success of her book *Little Women*. Mayor Frederick Lincoln lived at Number 19. William Dean Howells, an author and the editor of the *Atlantic Monthly*, lived at Number 4—to name just a few. Movie scenes from *Vanity Fair* by William Thackeray were taken in front of Number 20, allegedly with the help of two amateur actors, both residents of the square.

"BRAHMINS" ON THE SOUTH SLOPE

THE SUNNY South Slope attracted some of the wealthiest Bostonians of the nineteenth century, who soon became known as the Beacon Hill "Brahmins," a Sanskrit word for members of the priestly Hindu caste, the highest in the Hindu social hierarchy. The credit for applying this label in an American context is sometimes given to Oliver Wendell Holmes, Sr., the physician, writer, and social observer, himself a resident of Beacon Street. Unlike the Old World aristocrats, whose titles and status were the results of bloodlines, remarked Holmes, the Boston Brahmins were a caste of untitled aristocracy with houses by Bulfinch, who acquired a monopoly of Beacon Street, possessed ancestral portraits and Chinese porcelains, and espoused humanitarianism, Unitarian faith in the march of the mind, Yankee shrewdness, and New England exclusiveness.[16]

Oliver Wendell Holmes, Sr. (1809–1894), photogravure by A. W. Elson & Co. A poet and writer, Holmes coined the term "Boston Brahmin."

19

Indeed, on Holmes's own street, there had lived many a Yankee Brahmin. Harrison Gray Otis presided, for forty-two years, in his mansion at 45 Beacon, adjacent to the house he later built for his daughter, Sophia Ritchie. To the left of Sophia, in Number 42, lived Colonel David Sears, a son-in-law of Jonathan Mason. Further to the left, the textile king Nathan Appleton built Number 39 after selling Number 54 to his cousin William Appleton.

Over time, Mount Vernon and Chestnut Streets also held the "sifted few."[17] Senator Henry Cabot Lodge lived at 65 Mt. Vernon Street. A house at Number 26 was built for his daughter by the king of seafaring captains and shipping magnates, Colonel Thomas H. Perkins. Perkins, as the story goes, turned down an offer to become George Washington's secretary of the navy because he had to attend to his own collection of vessels, a fleet larger than that of the U.S. Navy.

On Chestnut Street, Hepzibah Swan, the only woman among the Mount Vernon Proprietors, built Numbers 13 through 17 for her three daughters, Christina, Sarah, and Hepzibah. These "daughter houses," pointed out Mrs. Swan, were commissioned for the advancement of her daughters, free and exempt from the control of husbands. Further down the street, Charles R. Codman, another successful sea captain, purchased Number 29A. The captain allegedly adorned his house entrance with a pair of white marble urns that once graced Malmaison, the château of the French empress Josephine.

Many of the Beacon Hill Brahmins had humble beginnings associated with sea trade; they gradually built fortunes through connections with the West Indies and China. On the sea, observed Cleveland Amory, everything

David Sears House, 1819. Courtesy of the Bostonian Society/ Old State House. Designed by Alexander Parris, the Sears House at 42 Beacon Street became the Somerset Club in 1872.

turned to gold, or at least silver, for the benefit of Boston merchants.[18] This was certainly true for Colonel Perkins of Mount Vernon Street and Captain Codman of Chestnut Street. The nouveaux-riches traders were joined on the South Slope by rising industrialists, as neighbors or by marriage, or both. Nathan Appleton, for example, made his fortune investing in the cotton mills built by Francis Lowell north of Boston. Together Appleton and Lowell founded a new industrial city named after Lowell.

During their heyday in the nineteenth century, the Beacon Hill Brahmins enjoyed a celebrated social life. In 1824, for instance, they wined and dined General Lafayette, loyal supporter of the American Revolution. In 1829 Harrison Gray Otis moved his mayoral inauguration from City Hall to his mansion on the Hill, where President James Monroe and Secretary of State Henry Clay were subsequently entertained. At 32 Mount Vernon Street, Dr. Samuel Gridley Howe, founder of the Perkins Institute for the Blind, and his wife, Julia Ward Howe, welcomed President Ulysses S. Grant. At 19 Louisburg Square, Mayor Frederick Lincoln honored the Prince of Wales, the future King Edward VII of England.

Leading literary lights also frequented the South Slope. The "daughter houses" were turned into highbrow literary salons. The house at 17 Chestnut Street, in particular, became a gathering place for the Transcendental philosophers Emerson and Whittier and the poets Longfellow and Holmes. Charles Dickens was also entertained by friends on the Hill, and he found Boston "a memorable and beloved spot."

The social doings on the South Slope during this period endowed Beacon Hill with a reputation of being the most affluent enclave in Boston. In the seventeenth century Governor Winthrop had promised that his social experiment was one on which the eyes of all people would fall. By the nineteenth century, Beacon Hill had indeed become the envy of many in America.

SLIDING FORTUNES

*B*EACON HILL's prominence suffered a severe blow when the landfill project of greater Boston led to the creation of high-end residences in the Back Bay and the South End. These projects were precipitated partly by Boston's rapid population growth between 1840 and the Civil War. In 1840 only 93,000 people lived in Boston; by 1860 the population almost doubled, reaching 178,000. In addition to the challenges of population growth, retail stores now encroached on residential districts, causing many urbanites to pack up and relocate to the country. Since Boston was limited in landmass and surrounded by water, it needed to find some way to add living space. The landfill project was the answer.

The first of these expansions began with the South Cove Corporation, founded in 1833. It took two decades to fill in seventy acres of marshland to create what is today's South End district. This opened a new era of investment, housing construction, and prosperity for the area and attracted affluent families to the newly built "brownstones" there. Success in the South End also encouraged planners to upgrade another marshland adjacent to Beacon Hill, the so-called Back Bay. The city commissioners approved the ambitious Back Bay development plan in 1857. Some of the city's best-known Brahmin families—with names like Lawrence, Forbes, Cabot, Saltonstall, and Standish—shared the city's new vision, offering to purchase lots for their new homes. They bargained with the Commonwealth of Massachusetts, hoping to acquire the land at prices below the minimum, arguing that they bore substantial risks in making the investment. The commissioners finally gave in. Bolstered by the investments of the leading Brahmins, public confidence in the Back Bay development soared. Land was sold as quickly as it was filled. Shortly thereafter, grand streets were laid out, and on them were erected hundreds of magnificent brownstones. As if overnight, a new city had arisen atop the marshland of Boston's Back Bay, rivaling, it was said, "the most sumptuous quarters of the cities of the Old World."[19]

As these "sumptuous quarters" and broad avenues enhanced the Back Bay, they also made the once-magnificent Beacon Hill look outmoded by comparison. At the time the Civil War broke out, Beacon Hill was still consid-

Acorn Street, 1890,
photograph by John W.
Robbins. Courtesy of
the Society for the Preservation of New England
Antiquities.

ered the most prestigious residential neighborhood in Boston. By the war's end, Beacon Hill was overshadowed by the South End and soon would be by the Back Bay. Construction in the Back Bay also benefited from the advances in domestic technology—from central heating systems and gas lighting to modern plumbing and sewage. In 1875 there began a migration, leading to the rise of Back Bay and the decline of Beacon Hill for the next thirty years.

The low point on Beacon Hill came in 1905, when real estate values plummeted. Attracted by lowered rents and higher vacancy rates, retail shops and clubs began to invade the Hill. The first floors of many houses on Beacon Street were converted into shops. Samuel Eliot Morison, the Harvard professor and historian, recalls growing up on Brimmer Street in this period, and how family maids used to say, "Master Sammy, do persuade your grandpa to move to a swell neighborhood, like Commonwealt' Avenoo."[20]

THE NORTH SLOPE

*B*EACON HILL's North Slope, an area between Pinckney and Cambridge Streets, was a poor cousin of the South Slope. The Hill's north side was much steeper, sloped toward the waterfront, and had no full exposure to the sun. Dubbed the "dark" side of the Hill, the North Slope developed sporadically and independently from the South. Many of the streets were unnumbered, lined by makeshift wooden sheds, even though some lots had been laid out on paper earlier than their counterparts on the South Slope.

On what is today's Myrtle Street, a small rope-making industry flourished in the early nineteenth century. The workmen, twisting the hemp around their waists, would walk backward a good distance along the street, creating "ropewalks" between Revere and Myrtle Streets. Hot pitch was then applied to the rope to preserve the yarn, sending pungent smells wafting through the neighborhood. The low rents of the North Slope attracted a transient population of sailors and laborers. It also won a reputation as "Mount Whoredom," the first "Combat Zone" in Boston, until Mayor Josiah Quincy forcibly cleansed the area. To separate the South Slope from the "corruption" of the

Children at the corner of Revere and Anderson Streets, 1890, photograph by John W. Robbins. Courtesy of the Society for the Preservation of New England Antiquities.

North Slope, the Mount Vernon Proprietors created a barrier with Pinckney Street, which had only two connecting streets between the north and south sides.

Houses that remained on the North Slope from the earlier times of settlement included homes of craftsmen such as bakers, shoemakers, and carpenters. Louis Glapion, a mulatto barber from the West Indies, and George Middleton, a black coachman who served in the American War of Independence, co-owned what became Numbers 5 and 7 Pinckney Street, built in the early 1790s, a decade before Pinckney Street was even laid out. The "little wooden house" changed hands many times, providing shelter to a succession of shoemakers until the end of the nineteenth century.

Halfway down the North Slope, from Pinckney Street to the foot of the Hill, there lived a community of African Americans. It was a community that would eventually bring international attention to the North Slope as the nation wrestled with the issue of slavery, first through political debate, then with arms.

The first known record of African Americans in Boston dates back to 1638, just eight years after Winthrop and his people moved to the Shawmut Peninsula. The population was small, with only four hundred people of African heritage living in Boston by 1708, half of them born in America. By the time the colonies emerged victorious in the War of Independence, the population of African Americans in Boston approached fifteen hundred.

Many of the earlier African Americans settled not on the North Slope of Beacon Hill, but in the North End of Boston, sometimes pejoratively dubbed "New Guinea." Many were buried there, separate from their white neighbors, in Copp's Hill Burying Ground, one of the oldest cemeteries in Boston. But population growth in the North End, along with deteriorating living conditions there in the late eighteenth and early nineteenth centuries, forced many African Americans to relocate on the farmland of Beacon Hill's North Slope, already the home to a few black families, dating back to 1760. At first, Joy Street attracted the majority of the new settlers. Some thirty years later many spread out to what are today Charles Street, Myrtle Street, and the so-called West End. By the mid-nineteenth century, 80 percent of Boston's African American population had moved to the North Slope of Beacon Hill and adjacent areas of the West End.

Most African American settlers took on work close to their neighborhood, whether as barbers, shoemakers, rope makers, or domestic servants to families on the South Slope. Several of them made an impact on American history. John Rock of 83 Phillips Street, originally a dentist, found his new calling in the study of law, and in 1866 became the first African American lawyer to try cases before the U.S. Supreme Court. John De Grasse, of 31 Charles Street, received an M.D. degree from Bowdoin College in 1849, and became a member of the Massachusetts Medical Society in 1854. He served bravely during the Civil War as assistant surgeon to the Thirty-fifth Colored Troops, and subsequently became the first African American commissioned as a surgeon in the U.S. Army.

Lewis Hayden of 66 Phillips Street became a legend of the Underground Railroad movement. Hayden had been born into slavery in Kentucky. He and his wife escaped through the Underground Railroad and lived in Canada before moving to Beacon Hill in the 1850s. Once in Boston, Hayden turned his home into a haven for fugitive slaves. When Harriet Beecher

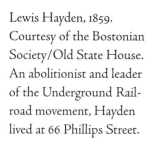

Lewis Hayden, 1859.
Courtesy of the Bostonian
Society/Old State House.
An abolitionist and leader
of the Underground Rail-
road movement, Hayden
lived at 66 Phillips Street.

Stowe, the author of *Uncle Tom's Cabin*, visited the Hayden house, some thirteen newly escaped slaves were brought into one room for her to see. At the entrance of the house, Hayden had stored piles of hidden gunpowder, ready at all times to blow the house up, should slave hunters arrive—even if fugitives were still inside. "We'd rather die free than be captured," claimed Hayden. An estimated seventy-five fugitives used Hayden's "underground station" on their way to freedom.

AMERICA'S FIRST BLACK CHURCH

*I*N THE seventeenth and eighteenth centuries, black churchgoers on the North Slope had been allowed to attend Baptist churches alongside whites. However, they were treated as second-class citizens, required to sit in church galleries where they could not see the preacher. In Boston slavery was

The exterior of the African Meeting House, 1885. Courtesy of the Society for the Preservation of New England Antiquities. This was the first African meetinghouse in the nation and the birthplace of the Anti-Slavery Society led by William Lloyd Garrison.

Smith Court, the home of the African Meeting House, photograph probably by John Robbins. Courtesy of the Society for the Preservation of New England Antiquities.

abolished in 1783, but even so, black Baptists were not given voting privileges in church. Over time, they envisioned establishing a church dedicated to African Americans. Encouraged by the African Society, a Boston organization formed in the early nineteenth century for the advancement of African Americans, blacks on the North Slope founded the First African Baptist Church on August 8, 1805.

The new church started with only twenty members and a pastor, the Reverend Thomas Paul. Initially the congregation made use of schoolhouses and other makeshift facilities for meetings and worship. A campaign to raise funds for a permanent meetinghouse was eventually launched, thanks to energetic leadership of the African Society and other community leaders. Donations began to pour in from supporters, black and white, all around the country. Finally, on December 6, 1806, the African Meeting House, the first black church in the nation, was dedicated at the corner of Smith Court and Joy Street and was immediately occupied by its first congregation, the First African Baptist.

For years the only facility available for educating black children was a room in the basement of the meetinghouse. In 1830, however, a white philanthropist named Abiel Smith left an endowment for black children's education. A school named after Abiel Smith was eventually founded in 1835 next to the meetinghouse, where parents paid 12½ cents per week for a child's education. The African Meeting House was first started to accommodate religious worship; eventually it would become a pivotal center in the political fight against slavery, earning itself the nickname "the colored people's Faneuil Hall."

THE FIGHT AGAINST SLAVERY

Early bostonians held mixed feelings about slavery. From the time of Winthrop there had been various initiatives to deal with the issue. "There shall never be any bond slaves or captive among us," stated the Massachusetts Body of Liberties in 1641, "unless it be lawful captive taken in just wars and such strangers as willingly sell themselves or are sold to us."[21] Actually, the Puritans had Indians in mind at the time, not blacks. The statement, however, left the door open for various interpretations. Some early Puritans advocated the economic benefit of slaves. "I do not see how we can thrive until we get in a stock of slaves sufficient to do all our business," wrote Emanuel Downing to his brother-in-law, Governor John Winthrop, arguing the need for cheap labor in the colony. Other citizens, however, voiced opposition. Citing the Scriptures, Judge Samuel Sewall, in *The Selling of Joseph*, attacked the institution of slavery and its continuation in Massachusetts.[22]

By the end of the Revolutionary War, the issue again came to the forefront in national consciousness and debate. The war provided ready-made rhetoric for the antislavery movement. If Americans felt they had been enslaved by British tyranny, how could they justify the bondage imposed on African slaves? It was a question the Worcester County slave Quock Walker used to challenge the Massachusetts Supreme Court to reexamine the state constitution's position on slavery. Chief Justice William Cushing, after much debate, stated that the constitution "by which the people of this commonwealth have solemnly bonded themselves sets out with declaring that all men are born free and equal." He concluded, "this being the case, I think the idea of slavery is inconsistent with our own conduct and Constitution; and there can be no such thing as perpetual servitude of a rational creature."[23] Cushing's judgment officially brought slavery to an end in Massachusetts in 1783.

Public opinion was, however, much divided. Not a few Bostonians sympathized with southern proponents of slavery. Others, including many of the older Beacon Hill Brahmins, were torn between their commercial interests, which seemed to depend on perpetuating slavery, and a humanitarian conscience, which called for abolition.

By the 1820s, economic interests between North and South were becoming increasingly intertwined, especially as seafaring trade receded and textile mills were established in Massachusetts. The more efficient the textile mills of Lawrence and Lowell became, the more dependent became their founders on the raw materials and markets provided by the South. There was an "unhallowed union," charged Charles Sumner, between the lords of the lash and the lords of the loom.

Abolitionism was an unpopular position among some Brahmin families of the South Slope. Harrison Gray Otis, for instance, was mayor of Boston when the abolitionist journal *The Liberator* was published. When urged to investigate its background, Otis predicted that the journal had not made, nor was it likely to make, converts among the respectable class. Many of his Beacon Hill neighbors shared his view. Nathan Appleton, for one, believed that slavery was a local problem for other parts of the country, and he would have nothing to do with abolitionists such as William Lloyd Garrison, seen by many as a "fanatical megalomaniac."[24]

But not all "respectable folks" on the Hill agreed with Otis and Appleton. The South Slope was home to leading abolitionist sympathizers, such as the Channings and the Adamses (of Mount Vernon Street), Joshua Dodge (of Chestnut Street), John Parkman (of Walnut Street), and Dr. Henry I. Bowditch (of Otis Place). Many of these Brahmin supporters, preferring a moderate approach at first, were pushed toward more radical positions as events unfolded.

The antislavery movement found its most effective advocate in the white abolitionist William Lloyd Garrison. On January 6, 1832, Garrison founded

Charles Sumner (1811–1874). Courtesy of the Boston Public Library. A U.S. senator and an abolitionist, Sumner was a resident of 20 Hancock Street.

the New-England Anti-Slavery Society at a rally held in the African Meeting House, after being denied the use of Faneuil Hall. Beacon Hill again became a focal point in the nation's consciousness, and the African Meeting House came to be called the "Abolitionist Church," in addition to its reputation as the colored people's Faneuil Hall.

William Lloyd Garrison
(1805–1879). Courtesy of
the Boston Public Library.
A fervent abolitionist, he
was the founder of the
abolitionist journal *The
Liberator*.

View of the Boston Common, by Christian Remick, c. 1768. Engraving by Sidney Smith. Courtesy of the Concord Museum. Across from the Common were what are believed to be the three Copley properties *(left)* and the Hancock Manor *(right)*.

Moving Mountains, chromolithograph by J. H. Bufford, from an 1811 watercolor by J. R. Smith. Courtesy of the Boston Public Library. The view is from Mount Vernon Street, with William Thurson's house in the background. Approximately sixty feet were removed from the top of the Hill.

Moving Mountains, chromolithograph by J. H. Bufford, from an 1811 watercolor by J. R. Smith. Courtesy of the Boston Public Library. The view is from Hancock and Temple Streets. Beacon Hill was being cut down to make room for the construction of residential buildings on the South Slope.

Beacon Hill, chromolithograph by J. H. Bufford, from an 1811 watercolor by J. R. Smith. Courtesy of the Boston Public Library. Beacon Hill is seen from Derne Street.

View of Beacon Street looking toward Charles Street, 1855, hand-colored wood engraving from *Ballou's Pictorial Boston.*

Church of the Advent, 1880s, from *King's Handbook of Boston*.

Beacon Hill and the Common from Arlington Street Church, 1872, hand-tinted wood engraving from *Picturesque America*.

View of the State House from the Common, 1892. Courtesy of the Bostonian Society/Old State House.

Garrison, together with his fellow abolitionists, virtually turned the Meeting House into a forum for the antislavery movement. At a meeting on January 6, 1832, he told his audience: "We hold that man cannot, consistently with reason, religion, and the eternal and immutable principles of justice, be the property of man. We hold that whoever retains his fellow man in bondage is guilty of a grievous wrong. We hold that a mere difference of complexion is no reason why any man should be deprived of any of his natural rights, or subjected to any political disability." He concluded with words that echoed across the Hill: "We have met tonight in this obscure school house; our numbers are few and our influence limited; but, mark my prediction, Faneuil Hall shall ere long echo with the principles we have set forth. We shall shake the Nation by their mighty power."[25]

Wendell Phillips (1811–1884). Courtesy of the Boston Public Library. He was an abolitionist and an effective orator for the antislavery movement.

William Lloyd Garrison did shake the nation. Even on the South Slope of Beacon Hill, he won over some of the most affluent families, especially the younger generations. Well endowed with education and inherited wealth, the children of these families bore the names of Phillips, Quincy, Loring, Chapman, Sewall, and Weston. Apparently the younger abolitionists discovered, in the antislavery movement, some of the same sense of fervor and purpose their forefathers mustered in the fight against British rule. Partly under the influence of Garrison, Edmund Quincy, a son of the second mayor of Boston, Josiah Quincy, shared and expanded on his father's apprehension about the impact of slavery on America's political consciousness. The American union, said Edmund, was "a confederacy with crime." Daughters of the Weston family saw in the abolitionist movement an opportunity for educated, upper-class women to participate in national politics, following in the footsteps of Abigail Adams from the previous generation. Wendell Phillips, a son of the first mayor of Boston and perhaps the most eloquent of the young abolitionists, found support for the immediate emancipation of slaves in both the Puritan tradition and the Revolutionary experience of John Hancock, Thomas Paine, and Samuel Adams. He took to task Beacon Hill's Brahmins, calling them "Old families run to respectable dullness. Snobbish sons of fathers lately rich, anxious to show themselves rotten before they are ripe."[26]

The Phillips House, c. 1890. Courtesy of the Boston Public Library. Designed by Charles Bulfinch, the Phillips House was built at the beginning of the nineteenth century at the corner of Beacon and Walnut Streets by John Phillips, Boston's first mayor. Wendell Phillips, his son, was born here.

But it was a catastrophic event in 1837 that finally united the more radical and the more conservative abolitionists—the murder of the Reverend Elijah P. Lovejoy by a proslavery mob in Alton, Illinois. Led by the Unitarian churchman William Ellery Channing, the abolitionists petitioned the city to use Faneuil Hall for a rally to register protest against the crime. When the mayor declined, a public outcry followed that brought together radical and moderate abolitionists and public-minded nonabolitionists in a common cause against the mayor. The mayor finally gave in. On December 8 the doors of historic Faneuil Hall, renowned as "the cradle of liberty" during the American Revolution, were thrown open and not a seat was left unfilled. Perhaps more than any other single event, this forged the abolitionist alliance.

By 1851 the alliance succeeded in getting its members elected to national office. Beacon Hill's Charles Sumner, an outspoken abolitionist and legal defender of several fugitive slaves, was elected to the U.S. Senate. To celebrate his victory, a hundred-gun salute was fired on the Boston Common. Throughout the city, churches of many denominations rang their bells. A spontaneous victory parade formed at the State House. Marchers, cheering and chanting, moved triumphantly through the streets of Beacon Hill, culminating their march at 20 Hancock Street, Sumner's house.

In the years that followed, the African Meeting House resonated with the words of new advocates emboldened by Garrison and Sumner, most notably the escaped slave Frederick Douglass. "Four millions have bowed before this nation," said Douglass on December 3, 1860, "and with lifted hands to Heaven and to you, have asked, in the name of God, and in the name of humanity, to break our chains."[27] By 1863, during the Civil War, the African Meeting House became a recruitment center for the Fifty-fourth Massachusetts Infantry, the first black regiment fighting for the Union, led by a native son of Beacon Hill, Colonel Robert Gould Shaw. Among Colonel Shaw's black soldiers were the two sons of Frederick Douglass, Charles and Lewis. On July 19, 1863, Colonel Shaw led the brave but fatal charge on Fort Wagner in Charleston, South Carolina, and was among the first to fall, followed by hundreds of his black comrades-in-arms. The courage of Shaw and his men was memorialized by the handsome bas-relief monument created by Augustus Saint-Gaudens, opposite the State House. Across Beacon Hill, and

The interior of the African Meeting House, 1937, photograph by Arthur Haskell. Courtesy of the Society for the Preservation of New England Antiquities. From about the turn of the century until 1972 the meetinghouse served as the synagogue of Congregation Libavitz.

especially on the North Slope, black activists conversed freely with white activists, now joined in a common purpose. For a moment in time, the color line on Beacon Hill blurred.

A decade after the Civil War ended, Beacon Hill witnessed an exodus of some wealthy families to the newly developed Back Bay. This was paralleled by an exodus of black families from the North Slope migrating to Roxbury, the South End, and other parts of Boston. Many ramshackle wood and brick houses that had sheltered the black population were torn down to make way for tenement housing. By the end of the nineteenth century, black families had virtually disappeared from the Hill, replaced by a succession of European immigrants. The African Meeting House was sold in 1898 and served as a place of worship for the Jewish community for the next seventy-four years. In an odd way, the end of the nineteenth century culminated eras for Brahmins and blacks alike.

BEACON HILL BOHEMIAN

*F*ROM QUITE EARLY TIMES, the North Slope, especially Pinckney Street, gained a reputation for being a "Bohemian" colony—populated by artists and writers, fond of its clear view of the Charles River, and blessed with low rents. The composer Lowell Mason lived at Number 9 in the 1830s. Edwin Whipple, an essayist and literary critic, lived at Number 11 for many years, followed by the novelist Alice Brown. Maturin Murray Ballou, an editor of several periodicals and newspapers, including *Gleason's Pictorial* and the *Boston Globe*, lived at Number 17 in 1847.

The erosion of Brahmin presence in the late 1860s gave rise to a second wave of artistic types, made possible by affordable rooming houses in what had been single-family structures. Pinckney Street continued its tradition as a young and vibrant literary nerve center. Nathaniel Hawthorne, Herman Melville, and Louisa May Alcott all found Pinckney Street a congenial place to live. Also drawn to the street was Bronson Alcott, the devoted follower of Ralph Waldo Emerson and the father of Louisa May Alcott. The house at 66 Pinckney, it was said, "offered hospitality to the disillusioned of the Brook Farm Commune,"[28] after the collapse of that Transcendental experiment. Also close by, at 3 Joy Street, lived Helen Clarke and Charlotte Potter, founders of the avant-garde journal *Poet Lore*, which claimed as one of its contributors a controversial figure of the time, Walt Whitman.

A third wave of "young Bohemians" settled on the North Slope during the last two decades of the nineteenth century. Like their predecessors, they were energetic, searching, and artistically gifted. According to the novelist Anna Farquhar, "There are to be found musicians; newspaper people; painters; incipient authors and a few full-fledged; impecunious youths with high spirits and one 'dress suit' among several . . . here is the freedom of the Latin Quarter.

Ralph Adams Cram
(1863–1942). Courtesy of
David Scudder. An archi-
tect and writer, Cram was
responsible for numerous
gothic structures, some of
which are at Princeton,
Williams, Phillips Exeter,
Rice, and West Point.

. . . In truth, this Boston Bohemia stands for good spirits and innocent un-
conventionality, and is several times more virtuous than Boston society."[29]

If anything separated this latter-day generation from their forebears, it
was their air of optimistic innocence. Unlike the Beacon Hill Bohemians of
the Civil War era, the new Bohemians lived in a period of postwar prosperity and relative peace. High hopes, definite ambitions, certainty of achieve-

ment, and lightness of heart created an atmosphere of which one could breathe deeply, Ralph Adams Cram, a leading Bohemian of Pinckney Street, reminisced forty years later. "There was no sign, no cloud, even the smallest, on the horizon of destiny; no indication (and fortunately) of the coming era of big business, mass production, and high finance, of labor wars, racketeering, gangsterism, and wholesale kidnapping. A war in which America would be involved—even a little one like that with Spain, then coming close—was unthinkable. As for a World War, exceeding in magnitude and devastation any of those in the past . . . the complete breakdown of our social, moral, and economic system . . . the maddest of us all would never have conceived anything of the kind."[30] In this age of innocence, as brief as it was, Beacon Hill youth did not share the radicalism and activism of the previous generation. There were no experimental commune members, no runaway slaves, just high hopes and a newfound camaraderie among fellow residents of the Hill.

Many, though, grew to become respected professionals. The architect Ralph Adams Cram designed, among others, the high altar credence of the Church of the Advent on Beacon Hill, the All Saints Church in Ashmont, Massachusetts, and the Cathedral of St. John the Divine in New York. Fred Holland Day, Cram's friend and Pinckney Street neighbor, became one of America's avant-garde photographers, whose sensational *Study of the Crucifixion* was almost a century ahead of Robert Mapplethorpe in the use of provocative nude forms. Day also included in his circle the young Kahlil Gibran, whose book *The Prophet* brought him international recognition. "We were," as Cram recalled later, "by instinct and inclination 'Beacon Hillites.' It was a closely-knit, intimately sympathetic community, with a real unity in tastes and ideas. The give-and-take social and intellectual traffic was in itself a true creative energy."[31]

Before long, however, the optimism, youthful gentility, and peace would be shattered by two world wars. A fundamental change occurred as the nation became preoccupied with issues that couldn't have been further from the minds of the young Boston idealists. Still, the past had left the Hill many legacies, from its Brahmins to its slave emancipators to its Bohemian "colonists"—a culturally rich and diverse foundation it would never lose.

CHAPTER TWO

The Beacon Hill Renaissance

1900–1930

Little shops, green grocers, meats,
Pastries, cobblers, spirits, sweets,
Rendezvous for daily shoppers,
Some in slacks and some in toppers.

MINA DEHART MIDDLETON
"Little Streets on Beacon Hill"

GRANDFATHER had often said to my father: Back Bay is man's land, but Beacon Hill is God's land, and by God they will come back to His land."[1] So remembered John Codman, a longtime Beacon Hill resident, realtor, and preservationist. It was this semireligious faith in the Hill, coupled with a keen entrepreneurial spirit, that encouraged a new group of "latter-day Mount Vernon Proprietors" to dedicate their lives to restoring Beacon Hill at the turn of the twentieth century.

Several events signaled the beginning of this rebirth. In 1905 the renowned architect Frank A. Bourne moved to Beacon Hill from Back Bay and purchased 130 Mount Vernon Street, the "Sunflower House," and resurrected it from deterioration. Five years later William Coombs Codman, a realtor and friend of Bourne, formed a real estate trust called the West End Associates, with the sole purpose of buying houses on streets such as Myrtle, Revere, and Pinckney. These he called the "firing lines," hoping to keep them out of the hands of greedy developers so they could be sold to persons who would appreciate them. Indeed, plenty of like-minded people, as William Codman soon discovered, appreciated his vision for renewal and subscribed to his West End Associates. Codman, with the profits from the sales, bought more apartments and turned them around for other qualified buyers, forming a "revolving fund," a popular strategy being adopted in the historic districts of other cities such as Charleston and Savannah. It was by no means a charitable trust; the original investors all made a handsome profit because, as they foresaw, Beacon Hill was turning a positive corner, and people were gradually coming back.

In 1917 William Codman formed another company that would power forward much of the renovation. Known as Beacon Hill Associates, its mission was to reinvigorate the North Slope and the West Slope, also called "the Flat,"[2] so that both slopes would be known as neighborhoods of first-class homes. Fortunately for the Hill, the Associates proved to be people of vision. They insisted on high architectural standards for renovation years before the city of Boston came to create zoning laws. All new buildings were to be made of red bricks in the Georgian revival style. This extended the traditional style of Beacon Hill structures onto the Flat, integrating that new area into the neighborhood as a whole.

OPPOSITE:
Beacon Hill, c. 1913, sketch by Ralph McLellan. Courtesy of the Beacon Hill Civic Association.

45

This masterstroke of historical preservation was made possible by the collaboration of like-minded architects. Frank Bourne and his colleague Dana Somes, both preservationist architects, designed Charles River Square, as well as new buildings on Brimmer Street between Chestnut and Lime Streets. Richard Arnold Fisher, another revivalist architect, designed 50–58 Brimmer Street and 62 Beacon Street. Altogether, the Beacon Hill Associates were responsible for four low-rise apartments and sixty single-family houses in the area. These were congenial collaborations, recalled John Codman.[3] In effect, the Beacon Hill Associates became to the Flat of the Hill what the Mount Vernon Proprietors were to the South Slope a century before.

William Codman and his partners at the Associates also realized early on the significance for the new Beacon Hill of its main promenade—Charles Street. As Charles Street went, they believed, so would the whole neighborhood. With a sense of urgency, they employed the same revolving fund strategy to acquire the "studio building" at the corner of Chestnut Street (Number 82 today) as well as 130 to 140 Charles Street. On his own, Codman developed the old Lincolnshire Hotel at 20 Charles Street and the commercial building at Number 30, which he turned into the Codman Company office. Even though Charles Street has gone through several other "face-lifts" since his time, Codman and his colleagues were the first ones to transform it.

Restoration efforts of the Associates triggered a chain of events on other parts of the Hill. A feature article in the *Boston Transcript* on August 21, 1926, described new developments on the back slopes as some of the most impressive in all of Greater Boston. Artistic interiors and delightful gardens replaced previously squalid tenements and dirty, foul-smelling alleys and streets. The article spotlighted rehabilitation at Primus Avenue, off Phillips Street, and Champney Place, off Anderson Street. These buildings, before the renovation, had no heat or electricity, and plumbing was substandard. Then came "the revolution," said the *Transcript*. William Codman and Elliott Henderson were among the first to see the possibilities of restoring the old buildings where the new gardens, as well as the quietness and convenience of the small suites, would appeal particularly to artists and those who worked downtown and desired a convenient, attractive place within easy reach.[4]

If rising real estate value is a measure of success, the Beacon Hill renaissance in the early twentieth century certainly turned things around. Between 1919 and 1924 the property values on the Hill increased by 24 percent, followed by another 25 percent gain from 1924 to 1929, according to the *Transcript*.[5] Beacon Hill "is coming back," also claimed the *Boston Sunday Advertiser*. Fifty years before, Beacon Hill had seen a tremendous exodus of those who disapproved of grocery stores and restaurants next door to their homes. But now there was an influx toward the Hill, and the wealthy four hundred families[6] were coming back. By the end of the 1920s, with Beacon Hill reborn, the Beacon Hill Associates dissolved, sensing their mission complete.

The twentieth-century "Mount Vernon Proprietors" shared much in common with their eighteenth-century predecessors. They were driven by a vision that, given some imaginative investment, Beacon Hill could have a far more significant future. It was this kind of vision that allowed them to see in Beacon Hill what others had missed. In Beacon Hill, the Mount Vernon Proprietors saw potential for a residential neighborhood that would take advantage of proximity to the new State House, as well as its "genteel and airy situations." The Beacon Hill Associates, for their part, recognized the intrinsic value of what restoration of the Flat and the North Slope could bring to the future of the entire Hill. Both groups also shared a keen entrepreneurial spirit. They were, above all, persons of business acumen who understood how to turn a simple idea into an enterprise of vitality.

"STREET-FIGHTER": MARIAN NICHOLS

ONE OF the oldest and most tenacious neighborhood associations in American history had a feisty start, thanks to some colorful characters of the Hill. This beginning involved a decision of the City of Boston to repave some of Beacon Hill's streets in shale paving blocks—hoping to prevent the old brick pavement from suffering further deterioration. The resurfacing was planned for October of 1920, starting with Mount Vernon Street. As word of the plan got out, a group of Beacon Hill neighbors hastily organized. On October 26 they stormed a Street Commission hearing to protest the city's decision. Shale pavement, they argued, would be too slippery for both horses and humans. As the *Boston Transcript* told the story, protesters claimed that Mount Vernon Street was unlike any other street in Boston, at least sentimentally, for this was a street with a history. City officials, they insisted, should not impose a street pavement that citizens detested. This landmark confrontation came to be remembered as "the First Battle of the Bricks," prefiguring several other such battles in the years to come. It was also the origin of the founding of the Beacon Hill Association. Three leaders in the battle became founders of the new association—Frank Bourne, William Codman, and Marian Nichols. Each brought to the association a unique background.

Marian Nichols, who exemplified a new generation of women activists, was later credited with the idea of founding a permanent neighborhood organization. The second of three daughters of an affluent Boston physician's family, Nichols spent much of her childhood and adult life at 55 Mount Vernon Street, which is now the Nichols Museum.[7] After a year of travel in Europe in her late teens, she entered Radcliffe College as a special student in 1898, having previously taken classes there.[8] Her time at Radcliffe was formative and implanted in Nichols a commitment to civic responsibility and causes of social justice. Her course in Forensics, she later recalled, "helped me to get the best in almost every argument with legislators at hearings."[9] The purpose and spirit of a Radcliffe education in those days were summed up in an address given by the Reverend Samuel M. Crothers, pastor of the First Parish Church of Cambridge, on the occasion of Nichols's commencement: to enlarge the mind and to increase the range of thought.[10]

Marian Nichols (1874–1963). Courtesy of the Shurcliff family. A reformer and activist, she was a founder of the Beacon Hill Association.

Marian Nichols typified college-educated women of America's Progressive Era, a period that witnessed the launch of urban and statewide reforms—legislation regulating railroads and public utilities, new compensation plans for injured workers, and renewal programs in urban slums.[11] Behind much of the activism were college-educated women who found their calling and place in American society through participation in social reforms. Marian Nichols was one of them, and she was one of the more tireless fighters.[12] With her high-spirited ways and strong-mindedness, Marian Nichols often found herself at odds with the Massachusetts Legislature. She would regularly walk to the State House, attending hearings, button-holing various officials, and inspecting government records. Possessing an indomitable spirit, recalled her nephew William Shurcliff, Marian would not be stopped by hints that she should forbear and sit down. Thanks to her keen mind, courage, and drive, she became an effective voice for the interests of women and countless civic groups, as well as the Beacon Hill neighborhood.

As legend has it, she once went to the State House for an appointment and was kept waiting for some time. Governor Leverett Saltonstall came to greet her and asked how she was. Marian Nichols replied, "I'm very tired of waiting to see you, and very cross to be kept waiting like this."[13] A few years earlier, She spearheaded a much-publicized political fight with the Women's City Club over the proposed addition to its Beacon Street clubhouse. To register her protest against the proposal, she resigned from the club in 1937.

In her various capacities, Nichols helped to recruit women for government service, fought for woman suffrage, and helped reform state legislation. In 1920 she ran, unsuccessfully, for state representative from the Beacon Hill District.[14] In 1945 she became the first woman member of the Council of the National Civil Service Reform League, and for seventeen years she served as executive secretary of the Beacon Hill Association. At the time of her death the *Boston Herald* called her a "life-long crusader for good government."[15] She herself described herself a little differently: "My chief interest has centered in fights at the State House, and my chief satisfaction has been to find right sometimes overcoming might."[16]

REAL ESTATE SAVVY: THE CODMANS

*W*ILLIAM C. CODMAN, another Beacon Hill Association founder, hailed from a local family renowned for its diverse involvements in real estate. His father, whose name also was William C. Codman, had begun in real estate in 1874 by launching a new real estate firm after his previous company, the Lawrence Fire Insurance Company, was forced into bankruptcy in the aftermath of Boston's Great Fire. The senior Codman lived for most of his life on West Cedar and later on Chestnut Street. William, his son, took over the family business in 1902 after an unsuccessful stint with importing. Both father and son shared a special passion for Beacon Hill, even though their business extended to the Back Bay and the South End.

In 1902 the junior Codman entered into a partnership with Gerald Street, an associate who started in the Codman company as an office boy, worked his way up, and became the right-hand man of Codman senior. This partnership, known as Codman and Street, would prove a profitable one. The firm promoted the new buildings that were constructed on lower Beacon Hill until approximately 1920. There were no zoning laws during those years, but the firm saw to it that good architects such as Richard Fisher, Dana Somes, and Frank Bourne designed the new to blend with the old.[17] The firm was dissolved in 1920 when Gerald Street formed his own firm, Street & Co.

In 1922 a third-generation Codman, John, joined his father's firm (now under the name William Codman & Son) after graduating from Harvard.

John Codman (1899–1989). Courtesy of the Codman family. The realtor and preservationist resided at 74½ Pinckney Street.

John Codman. Courtesy of the Codman family.

Like his father, John had acquired a deep sense of commitment to historic preservation. William, who had served as a director of the Beacon Hill Association during its early days, "wished" his seat on the association's Executive Committee to his son in 1937; he passed away the next year. John continued the family legacy on the Hill and made two major contributions to the district during his active career. In the 1950s he initiated a process that eventually turned Beacon Hill into a "Historic District," one of a handful in the nation at the time. This designation permanently protected the Hill from commercial encroachment and greedy developers. Under his leadership, the Beacon Hill Architectural Commission was created, moving John Codman and Beacon Hill into the forefront of a nationwide preservation movement.

In 1960 John also helped establish an organization dedicated to historic preservation, appropriately entitled Historic Boston. Under Codman's prodding as president from 1978 to 1981, wrote the *HBI Report*,[18] Historic Boston enlarged its original focus on the Old Corner Bookstore building to become a citywide revolving fund working with a wide array of organizations and projects.[19] It assisted with the renovation of the Arlington Street Church, the restoration of the Old Corner Bookstore, and the repair of the Austin Block in Charlestown.

John Codman's love of the city life was matched only by his devotion to the great outdoors. As a member of the Union Boat Club, he sculled on the Charles River well into his seventies. From their Maine summer home, John and his wife, Anna, canoed "over any unpolluted streams we can find," as he put it.

In the city he led an active life, serving on the Executive Committee of the Good Government Association, as chairman of the Boston Real Estate Exchange, as well as director of the Boston Center for Adult Education and the Beacon Hill Association. John Codman lived for forty years at 74½ Pinckney Street (known as the "Hidden House") until his death in 1989 at the age of ninety. Many neighbors still remember him "patrolling" up and down the Hill in his later years, looking for violations of the zoning law. Always accompanying him on these walks was his wire-haired terrier, Zodiac, likewise advanced in age but equally vigilant in the patrols.

Historic preservation remained John Codman's biggest passion. Even as the toll of aging was gaining control over his interaction with the rest of the world, recalled his family and friends, John's commitment to preservation was as strong as it had ever been during the prime of his life. One evening at dinnertime, a year before his death, John refused to leave the television news he was watching. Unable to speak, he was glued to the program, to the surprise of everyone around. As it turned out, there was a report on the latest development in preservation issues of Greater Portland. John would not miss an opportunity to keep up with the world of historic preservation. "The human spirit is a powerful thing," remarked Stanley Smith, director of Historic Boston, at John Codman's funeral, "even when our bodies and minds begin to lose some of their resiliency and effectiveness."[20]

ARCHITECTURAL PASSION: FRANK A. BOURNE

*F*RANK A. BOURNE, another founder and catalyst for Beacon Hill's renaissance, spearheaded a more general return of wealthy families from the Back Bay. An accomplished architect, he served for many years as a pro bono architect for the restoration of the Charles Street Meeting House, as a member of the Beacon Hill Association's Executive Committee, and as chairman of the Zoning Committee between 1922 and his untimely death in 1936. Bourne brought architectural insight and conservationist passion to the association. One of the principal objectives of the Beacon Hill Association, he explained in 1925, was the maintenance of this district as a homelike neigh-

Frank and Gertrude Bourne. Courtesy of the Beacon Hill Civic Association. Frank Bourne was an architect, preservationist, and founder of the Beacon Hill Association. Gertrude Bourne was a painter and the first president of the Beacon Hill Garden Club.

borhood. Later he wrote that a man should not expect to profit by selling to an undesirable buyer at the expense of his neighbors; speculators should go elsewhere for their profits. It was this kind of passion for the neighborhood that endeared Frank Bourne to his colleagues and fellow residents.

Bourne's wife, Gertrude, also shared this love for the Hill. An energetic woman and an accomplished watercolorist, Gertrude Bourne became a founder of the Beacon Hill Garden Club and served as its first president between 1929 and 1931. The Bournes opened their garden behind the "Sunflower House" for the club's first "Hidden Gardens of Beacon Hill" tour in 1929. Visitors taking the tours found the Bournes' hidden garden a delight, with its thatch-roofed birdhouse and circular stone fountain. The famed tour continues today. The proceeds, as agreed by association members, have gone to worthy causes such as the British war relief effort during World War II and renovation of the Public Garden.

LAUNCHING THE BEACON HILL ASSOCIATION

On a spring day in 1922, a few months after the First Battle of the Bricks, a meeting was held at Marian Nichols's home, 55 Mount Vernon Street. In retrospect, John Codman recalled, this marked the turning point for the new Beacon Hill. The economic downturn in postwar America was over and the boom of the 1920s had started to gain momentum. With parasitic real estate developers waiting in the wings, it was obvious to those attending that a permanent civic organization would be necessary to solidify the gains of the past and to design a better future. The organizational groundwork was laid for what would be the official launch later that year of one of the oldest neighborhood associations in America.

On December 4, 1922, at four o'clock, seventy-seven new members and guests gathered in a large assembly room on the fifth floor of 3 Joy Street, headquarters of the Twentieth Century Club, an organization established in 1894 to "promote a finer public spirit and better social order." Grace Minns, vice president of the new Beacon Hill Association, called the meeting to order. Marian Nichols, secretary, spoke next about the impetus that led to the formation of the organization and outlined some proposed goals and plans.

Among other speakers, Arthur Comey, zoning director for the Boston City Planning Board, discussed the zoning situation in Boston. So marked the birth of the Beacon Hill Association.[21]

A GENTLEMAN AND A "BULL DOG": ARTHUR D. HILL

*T*HE ASSOCIATION could not have wished for a more capable first president than Arthur D. Hill. He was born in Paris in 1869 to Adams Hill, a professor of English at Harvard, and Caroline Dehon Hill. The Hills were a New England family of "scholars, bookworms, and bluebloods." The family returned to Cambridge, Massachusetts, when he was three years old. While living in Cambridge, Arthur attended the Brown and Nichols School, and later the Harvard Law School, graduating in 1894, when he married Henrietta McLean of Bellport, Rhode Island.

Arthur Hill (1869–1947) at work. Courtesy of the Portsmouth Athenaeum, Wilson Collection. Arthur Hill was a founder of the law firm Hill & Barlow and a resident of Brimmer Street.

Arthur Hill was a founder of the law firm Hill & Barlow and served briefly but effectively as Suffolk County District Attorney. Between 1917 and 1919 he served in France in the Judge Advocate's Department of the U.S. Army. After the war he served for three years as legal counsel for the City of Boston before returning to full-time private practice.

Friends and neighbors of Arthur Hill came to think highly of him, among them the family of the author and literary critic Mark A. DeWolfe Howe, who lived near Hill on Brimmer Street. Arthur Hill was a "Simon-pure Yankee at its best," wrote Howe's daughter, Helen. "He came honorably by his wits and his wit," she said. "There was a continual warfare being waged between his tart, shrewd lawyer's mind and a tender heart. Sandy in coloring, with a high, thoughtful brow, and something of a scholar's stoop, he gave no appearance of being out of the ordinary. . . . I think it doubtful that New England has produced a finer example of its best breed. I am sure that there was no finer in Brimmer Street."[22]

Hill brought to bear his "shrewd lawyer's mind and a tender heart" most famously in the much publicized Sacco-Vanzetti case. Nicola Sacco and Bartolomeo Vanzetti, two Italian immigrants, were arrested on May 5, 1920, on suspicion of murder in South Braintree, Massachusetts. The nation was caught up in fears about communism after the Russian Revolution. The Italians were charged on slim evidence and did not seem likely to have a fair trial. Arthur Hill accepted the case as their last counsel in 1927, urged on by his colleague and a Beacon Hill neighbor, Felix Frankfurter. It was not a move that would endear Hill to the wider community. Many fellow members of the Somerset Club avoided him and generally gave him a cold shoulder. This public rebuff only fueled his courage, as he later explained: "If the president of the biggest bank in Boston came to me and said his wife had been convicted of murder, but he wanted me to see if there was any possible relief in the Supreme Court of the United States and offered me a fee of fifty thousand dollars to make such an effort, of course I would take the retainer. . . . I do not see how I can decline a similar effort on behalf of Sacco and Vanzetti simply because they are poor devils against whom the feeling of the community is so strong and they have no money with which to hire me. I don't particularly enjoy the proceedings that will follow but I don't see how I can possibly refuse to make the effort."[23] The fact that the men had not been given a fair trial under the law, reported Helen Howe, was enough for the fighting bulldog in him to dig his teeth into the cause of the oppressed, and not let go.[24] Hill lost the case. Sacco and Vanzetti were executed on August 23, 1927. He won much respect, however, from within the legal community and eventually from the public in later years.

Arthur Hill took seriously the presidency of the Beacon Hill Association, despite heavy demands from other professional engagements and obligations. He presided at nearly every meeting of the association during his tenure as president between 1923 and 1925, and he often became the spokesperson for the neighborhood at City Hall hearings. During his years as president, the membership of the association grew from 85 to 410. When Hill first took office on December 1, 1923, the association published a mission statement outlining goals and plans. The Beacon Hill Association, the statement said, believed it was for the best interests of the City of Boston as a whole, as well as for the good of the neighborhood itself, to have Beacon Hill preserved as a place of residence, with dwellings of the character prevailing today, free from additional business.

DEVELOPERS, BEWARE

THE ASSOCIATION'S focus on zoning in 1923 could not have been timelier. Concurrent to the association's efforts, the City of Boston was drafting its first comprehensive zoning law. Realizing the importance of inclusion and protection under this law, members of the association acted quickly. Educating residents was the first step, for which they invited zoning experts to speak at Association meetings. They also engaged the Murray Hill Association of New York to evaluate zoning issues on Beacon Hill, and they set up a permanent zoning committee under the chairmanship of Frank Bourne. Within eight months, the committee submitted several farsighted recommendations to the association.[25] When the city's first zoning ordinance became law in March the following year, almost all the recommendations of the association were included.

Height of Beacon Hill, c. 1930. Courtesy of the Beacon Hill Civic Association. Residents of Beacon Hill fought for decades to keep the building height limit at sixty-five feet for the entire district.

The inexperience of the association showed in several mistakes, however, which took another decade to undo. Phillips Street was left out of the association's initial zoning consideration. Already dotted with some small shops, the street was zoned by the city in 1924 for business, making it possible for more shops to crowd in from Charles and Cambridge Streets, threatening the residential nature of Beacon Hill's northern frontier. At the urging of Frank Bourne, the association petitioned the city to reclassify Phillips Street as a residential district. After much debate, the city granted the association's request, undoing the first oversight.

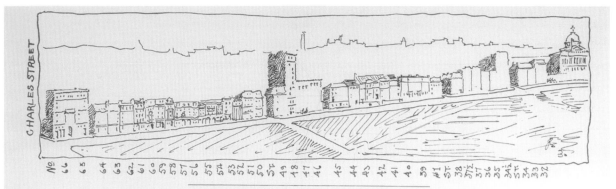

BEACON STREET HEIGHT LIMIT OPPOSITE BOSTON COMMON

With the growing tendency toward increasing the heights of buildings in different sections of the City, the Beacon Hill Association through its Zoning Committee has given much thought and study to the subject as it may affect Beacon Hill unless prompt action is taken to establish low building heights throughout this particular section.

It is felt that to allow high buildings to be erected on Beacon Street opposite the Common would be a fatal step toward destroying the charm of this neighborhood which is such a valuable asset to the City not only from the local but from the nation-wide point of view.

The Beacon Hill Association, in conjunction with a large number of property owners, is petitioning the Board of Zoning Adjustment to change the height limit on Beacon Street from Charles to Joy Street and Joy Street from Beacon to Myrtle Street from the present height of eighty feet to sixty-five feet which is now the height limit for the other streets on Beacon Hill from the State House to the Charles River—to the great material advantage of this unique residential district.

3 JOY STREET, BOSTON
March, 1930

The second mistake proved to be much more difficult to repair. The city's zoning law of 1924 failed to include Joy and Beacon Streets into either its residential designation or sixty-five-foot height restriction. Though the association was aware of the omissions, it took no action to remedy the situation, realizing only later how serious the matter was. In June 1928 the association was informed of a permit issued to the Episcopal Diocesan Council for an addition to its Diocesan House at One Joy Street. This permit would enable the council to have an eighty-foot tall, six-story building. Alarmed neighbors immediately formed a special committee to protest the intrusion and tried to bring the issue to Bishop Slattery of the Diocesan Council. The Beacon Hill Association itself took no active role other than issuing a mild statement. Bishop Slattery was not persuaded, and by the end of the summer many neighbors felt they had exhausted their Christian patience.

On October 9, 1928, over three hundred residents gathered at the Twentieth Century Club to express their opposition to the addition. Recognizing they had no legal ground on which to stand, the residents tried to appeal to the intelligence and conscience of every member of the Episcopal Diocese of Massachusetts. The *Boston Globe* reported the next day that the crowd's expressions of its sentiments ran the gamut from very dignified to very vehement.[26] Moderates, such as Greeley Curtis, recommended a campaign of education for church members. Another group, led by his sister, Frances, president of the Women's City Club, suggested that other property owners collaborate to buy the whole diocesan property. A more vehement contingent urged neighbors to build a brick wall on their various properties around the Diocesan House addition to shut off its light and ventilation. This block was the heart of Old Boston, said Edward T. Hartman, a state consultant for housing and town planning, and its proximity to the State House made the property unique. The addition would be an encroachment and an intrusion. "An old resident of the hill recently told me that these people must have copper-riveted souls to foster such a project."[27]

After hours of debate and letting off steam, the group finally accepted the recommendation of Greeley Curtis to implore members and authorities of the Episcopal Church to join with the neighbors in improving the historic neighborhood and to avoid leaving a permanent blot on the city and further embittering citizens. The neighbors lost their battle, and the addition was built onto the Diocesan House. Association members were not finished, however. In December 1928 Frank Bourne urged the Executive Committee to have Joy Street and Beacon Street, from the State House to Charles Street, included in Beacon Hill's sixty-five-foot height-limit.[28] After ten years and many painful fights, the city finally included all of Beacon Street within the sixty-five-foot zone.

On various occasions, the association was forced to defend this dearly fought victory. One challenge involved the Old Ladies Home lot between lower Pinckney and Revere Streets on Embankment Road. The home had been created through a bequest in 1861 as "an asylum for respectable aged women in straitened circumstance." In 1926 the elderly women were moved to a new facility in Jamaica Plain, leaving the building empty and the home's valuable fifty-six-thousand-square-foot parcel of land up for sale. Several developers had their eyes on the land, hoping to erect an apartment complex. The first proposal came from a Cambridge development group; it involved eight attached buildings, each with six stories and a penthouse. This translated into a seventy-foot-high complex, five feet taller than the sixty-five-foot zoning limit.

Frank Bourne, in a letter to the secretary of the association, Marian Nichols, sounded the battle cry. This was the first time that the zoning restrictions for Beacon Hill, as recommended and unanimously supported by the Beacon Hill Association, had been attacked. One of the principal objectives of the association, continued Bourne, was the maintenance of this district as a neighborhood of single-family homes. This was an important distinction for Frank Bourne and the association, whose members were primarily owners of single-family houses, which, argued Bourne, were distinctly the homes of citizens. Apartments were apt to house a migratory population. Zoning on Beacon Hill "protects the minority of owners of single-family houses against the large number of people who would come in if apartment houses increase on the Hill."[29] Many times throughout its history, the association would be accused of representing the interests of the affluent minority on the Hill. To the founders of the association, however, there was nothing wrong with standing up for single-family home owners since, to them, it was these owners who brought permanency and value to the Hill.

William Codman also sounded alarms over the new development proposal. He called it an "entering wedge" that would bring other petitions for increased building heights in other properties. If allowed, this would seriously threaten the future of Beacon Hill. Members of the association quickly mobilized to fight back, and during the fall, as Frank Bourne later wrote, Beacon Hill "moved down to City Hall," filling the hearing room of the Board of Zoning Adjustment. During these proceedings, the petitioner faced an array of the best legal minds in Boston arguing the case of home owners on the Hill.[30] No permission was granted and the development proposal was put aside for the time being.

The following year, however, developers returned with a still more ambitious plan.[31] Now they envisioned a five-million-dollar apartment hotel of fifteen stories, rising to a height of 155 feet. Moreover, developers had themselves enlisted formidable lawyers to argue their case at City Hall, among them a former attorney general. Once again, the association mobilized, turning the entire process into a successful neighborhood campaign, this time employing the mass media. A Zoning Defense Committee was formed. The committee drafted a flyer, entitled "The Menace to Beacon Hill," which included two mock-up photographs with close-up and distant views of Beacon Hill's riverfront. In the center of the traditional district appeared a dark, massive cube scaled to the proposed height of 155 feet. This frightening image was accompanied by a warning in block letters, "THE INTERESTS OF THE HILL ARE AT STAKE." If the development petition was approved, argued the committee, these splendid views toward and from the Hill would be lost, its residences would be dwarfed and shadowed by apartment buildings, or demolished to form parts of other large buildings, and the entire character of the Hill would be sacrificed. "Add the weight of your protest by attending the hearing on Friday," urged the committee. The pamphlet ended again with bold letters, "THE SITUATION IS SERIOUS—ACT."

The opposition's "big gun," the former attorney general J. Weston Allen, argued that instead of injury to nearby property the hotel would help it financially, citing similar hotels on Lake Shore Drive in Chicago and Riverside Drive in New York City. Furthermore, he said, the venture could not be a paying proposition unless it rose to 155 feet. The city's building commissioner added that he knew of twenty million dollars worth of buildings that would be located on Beacon Street if the restriction was removed.

On the afternoon of January 7, 1927, the hearing room of the Street Commissioners at City Hall was bursting with Beacon Hill residents protesting the building proposal. Representatives from the Massachusetts General Hospital and the Boston Society of Architects joined in speaking out against the plan. When it came time to vote, 214 people voted against raising the height limit, and only six voted in favor. And while there followed some talk among developers about filing an appeal to the state Supreme Court, the issue was dropped altogether when the Depression set in a few years later.

Once all of Beacon Hill came under the protection of the sixty-five-foot limit, the remaining years of the 1930s were relatively quiet on the zoning front. The mood on the Hill, as with the rest of the nation, had changed. The woes of economic depression demanded attention, as did the subsequent onset of another world war.

A TALE OF TWO MAIN STREETS

BEACON HILL has been blessed with not one but two "main streets"— Charles and Cambridge. Of the two, Cambridge Street is the elder, its origin going all the way back to 1647. It flanks the North Slope of the Hill, running westward to the Charles River. The street took its name in 1708, for it leads toward the city of Cambridge across the Charles River. Only later did it become a major thoroughfare between the two cities, when the West Boston Bridge was constructed in 1793. The bridge was renamed Longfellow in 1927, after the poet, who, legend had it, once stood on the bridge at midnight when the clock was striking the hour and later wrote a poem about the experience.[32]

Cambridge Street, from its humble beginning in colonial days as a cow path, later became a country road. In the nineteenth century, many of Boston's more illustrious citizens built mansions along the street, starting with Harrison Gray Otis. Otis built the first of his three houses in 1796 as an anniversary gift to his wife, the former Sally Foster, a proclaimed beauty in her day. Next door was the historic West Church, built in 1806 by Asher Benjamin, a friend and contemporary of Charles Bulfinch.[33] By the start of the twentieth century, however, Cambridge Street had become an avenue of small shops, primarily serving immigrants on the North Slope and the West End. It was a reminder that, after all, the great city now comprised a collection of neighborhoods more or less distinct. These neighborhoods, as the *Boston Evening Transcript* explained, served to show how people who would make Cambridge Street "their main street" might pass a lifetime and never penetrate the neighborhoods that lay beyond. Here they could find employment and all that was necessary to provide decent if not luxurious living.[34]

Indeed, in those days people tended not to venture beyond their neighborhood, especially when it came to the two slopes of the Hill. Residents of the South Slope considered Charles Street their main street. Access to the North Slope was somewhat blocked by Pinckney Street in between, as there were only two connecting streets linking the two slopes, West Cedar Street and Joy Street. By choice and by design, South Slope residents in those days rarely crossed over to the north side, with its heterogeneous communities, which included their servants. The North Slope communities, together with their West End neighbors, who shared much culturally, tended to consider Cambridge Street their own main street, where they found places to shop, socialize, and work.

In 1923 Mayor James Michael Curley initiated a $3.5-million-dollar plan to widen Cambridge Street from forty to one hundred feet in order to alleviate increased traffic. This project would affect 130 properties along the street, including the Otis House and other historical sites. Though the plan met with some opposition, most Beacon Hillers favored it. The Beacon Hill Association, which did not involve itself in Cambridge Street affairs as much as it did those of Charles Street, voted in favor of the mayor's initiative, but only after registering concern over the future of the Otis House. It took two years for the city to complete the project.

Cambridge Street's younger cousin, Charles, went through some changes of its own. Originally it had been created from landfill, with gravel and dirt from the Tri-Mountains. It was fifty-five-feet wide and was considered a link to the bridge, a convenient connector rather than an artery for traffic. In 1920

The widening of Cambridge Street as seen from Bowdoin Square, 1926. Courtesy of the Society for the Preservation of New England Antiquities.

the street was widened, with ten feet added to the section between Revere and Beacon Streets on the river side. By the late 1920s, however, the street again overflowed with traffic. "Charles Street," complained a resident to the *Boston Herald*, "is an impassable roaring river of traffic. Beacon Hill residents would like to walk to the Esplanade. I do not dare to risk the crossing. The shock of dodging the 'engines of death' is too great."[35] These engines of death not only made Charles Street impassable but also left it filled with dirt and mud.

At the 1928 annual meeting of the Beacon Hill Association, William Codman developed a resolution for the mayor, including ten requests and a rationale. Charles Street, declared the resolution, bordered the best residential district in the city, but was now harmed by the worst traffic. The association asked the city to divert heavy trucking to downtown streets, add lighting, remove rail tracks, and open a new station on the Cambridge subway line at the corner of Charles and Cambridge Streets. In two years, the association added, the city would host a tercentenary celebration, bringing thousands of visitors to the city. Surely, historic Beacon Hill should be in good order by then.

The idea of locating a subway station at the Charles-Cambridge corner was actually older than the association itself. In 1923 the association appointed a panel of distinguished citizens to monitor the subway issue and represent the association to the city. Chaired by Henry P. Kendall, a respected businessman, the group included Arthur D. Hill, March Bennett, and Bernard J. Rothwell. A subway station, claimed the association, was necessary for the convenience of the public, and immediate steps should be

Charles Street widening, 1920, photograph by W. T. Clark. Courtesy of the Society for the Preservation of New England Antiquities. In order to accommodate increased traffic on Beacon Hill, Charles Street was widened by about ten feet between Revere and Beacon Streets. The issue of traffic seemed all but resolved.

taken to erect the station.[36] No such steps were taken, however, as the proposal ran into continuous obstacles, including the efforts of representatives from the city of Cambridge, claiming that such a stop would delay the train for Cambridge commuters. In 1928 Governor Fuller also derailed the proposal with his veto.

The association, through its able advocates and partners, including Massachusetts General Hospital and several other institutions, kept coming back with the idea. By 1930 the tide began to turn. An impetus came from the scheduled widening of Charles Street and the building of a traffic circle, expected to be 240 feet in diameter, at the intersection of Cambridge and Charles Streets—a plan that now seemed to make construction of a subway station a legitimate public investment. Construction ensued the following summer. On February 28, 1932, the new station at Charles Circle opened to the public.

ENTER THE AUTOMOBILE

THE INTERNAL COMBUSTION ENGINE, observed the historian Samuel Eliot Morison, turned America's economy upside down and placed society on a completely new basis. Morison's own life spanned the transition from horse to car. Morison wrote with nostalgia about the days when the horse was dominant on the Hill. In fact, Chestnut Street between Charles Street and the river was called "Horse-Chestnut Street," since the Flat of the Hill was then lined with stables and harness and blacksmith shops. From seven o'clock in the morning to late afternoon, the cheerful ring of hammer on anvil could be heard. On Chestnut, many beautiful winter sleighs were built.[37] Sitting at his ancestral home on Brimmer Street in his later years, Morison reminisced about having his gray gelding, Blanco, at the Beacon Club Stable nearby, ready for his daily ride back and forth to Harvard. Tying Blanco to a tree in Harvard Yard, Morison would teach his classes, then return to load Blanco's saddlebags with student papers to be corrected at home. Even as late as 1900 the streets of Beacon Hill still belonged to the four-legged animals. A fleet of closed electric taxicabs first arrived in 1901.

Nicknamed "elephants on dumbbells" by the local residents, the electric cabs were huge and clumsy and did not last very long.

Whether Morison was ready for it or not, the automobiles would inexorably come. Ever since the introduction of railroads in Europe and America, human fascination had grown over the possibility of putting engines on wheels. Europeans led the charge during the 1870s, as French and German engineers experimented with gas engines. In 1893 the Duryea brothers built and operated the first gasoline-driven motor vehicle. It was Henry Ford's 1914 innovation, however, that made mass production possible—replacing stationary assembly with a moving assembly. Ford's idea cut the base price of a Model-T car from 950 to 290 dollars. Mass marketing was now assured. In 1895 only four automobiles traversed American highways; by the time America entered World War I in 1917 there were five million; and by the time the war ended, the number had grown to twenty-three million. Ford's innovation effectively made ownership possible well beyond the upper class.

With all the excitement about added speed and efficiency, some Americans started to worry that the machine was beginning to take over their lives. In addition to the noise and pollution of autos, many American streets were too narrow and fragile to handle the surge of new traffic. The number of accidents was increasing, parking became a nightmare, and congestion suffocated neighborhoods. Perhaps nowhere else were these conditions more painfully felt than on Beacon Hill, where the ancient streets had been designed for horses and buggies. Now the Hill, for hours in the afternoon, seemed to be turning into an open-air garage for cars unable to move forward or back. The Hill was turned into a thoroughfare and speedway for more than 140,000 cars that poured in and out of Boston daily.[38] To exacerbate the situation, the city in the summer of 1923 was planning to remove the sidewalk along Boston Common to create angled parking for 450 suburban vehicles. To turn this border of the Common into a parking lot was to threaten to deface one of the most picturesque locales in Boston. After the citizens protested, the city finally withdrew its plan.

As parking became a growing problem on the Hill, both residents and the city began to generate ideas to resolve it, ideas that seemed to come and go, only to resurface again later in the century. One such idea involved building

Autos parked on Charles Street, 1927, photograph by Leslie Jones. Courtesy of the Boston Public Library. The age of the automobile forever changed the colonial atmosphere of Beacon Hill streets.

an underground garage at the Common. This idea was quickly abandoned, but it resurfaced in the 1950s and became a reality. Another proposal involved establishing residential parking for Beacon Hill. Often residents of the area found their streets and parking spaces taken over by commuters, including legislators working at the State House. Residential parking, first proposed in

1923, actually materialized some fifty years later. In the meantime, Beacon Hill residents secured a number of garages to handle parking on the Hill.[39] And throughout the 1920s and 1930s Beacon Hillers fought the invasion of automobiles. In 1930 they turned seven streets into one-way streets in an effort to reduce traffic and accidents. In the 1930s they also petitioned the city to install automatic traffic signals at the intersections of major streets.

In 1933, when the association celebrated its tenth anniversary, Marian Nichols reflected on its achievements, including those for dealing with traffic. Charles and Cambridge streets had been successfully redesigned and widened, she said, while the Cambridge and Charles Street Elevated Station was proving its convenience. "Every effort to put up high buildings against our wishes had been defeated, except for one," she added, "and that very defeat had perhaps led to our outstanding constructive achievement of bringing Beacon Street opposite the Boston Common within the 65-foot limit." The parking situation had been improved through parking restrictions, one-way streets, and traffic lights on Charles Street. The battle would go on, however, as Nichols quickly pointed out. "Traffic problems are still a challenge and attempted infractions of the zoning law require our eternal vigilance." Indeed, no sooner had Charles Street been widened than it was constantly jammed by traffic. The widening of Cambridge Street also led to massive congestion at the Charles Street intersection. Beacon Hill residents would have to direct some of their vigilance permanently toward managing the necessary evils of the motorcar.

THE "LOST GENERATION"

THE ERA of World War I has been characterized as "America's Coming of Age."[40] Yet the "war to make the world safe for democracy," as President Woodrow Wilson called it, turned out to be a senseless slaughter. As young soldiers returned from the war and settled into the new decade, they were severely disillusioned, both about the world at large and the world at home. At home they found rising disparity between the haves and the have-nots, even though the national economy was starting to boom. Commercialism was replacing traditional values. As they looked over the state of the world, they were also disenchanted by failed promises. In their disenchantment they called into question conventional ideals and institutions. They came to be known as the lost generation. Artists and writers among their ranks shunned the new consumer society of the 1920s, seeking instead experimentation in defying Prohibition and other social constraints.

In Boston, members of this lost generation found their home on the North Slope of Beacon Hill, where previous groups of artists had traditionally congregated. In his book *Boston and the Boston Legend*, Lucius Beebe observed that "Boston's Greenwich Village sprang by a process of unpredicted and emergent evolution, into sudden, raucous and boozy being with the arts for an indifferent warrant and garret to garret hey-hey as leitmotiv." Overnight, he said, large numbers of previously rational and plausible youths and maidens discovered James Joyce and the formula for synthetic gin. They were fueled by the "disillusionment, Bohemia, and beautiful letters that arrived with nice precision in Boston after the World War."[41]

As if overnight, Beacon Hill came to be "invaded" by a free-spirited band of poets, actors, artists, and hangers-on. Joy Street became the nerve center of this community. On November 22, 1922, a small experimental theater, the Barn Theater, opened its doors in a converted stable at number 36 Joy Street. The play of the day was *The Clouds* by Jaroslav Kvapil, a Czech composer of whom very few Bostonians had ever heard. The stable and an adjacent strip of land had been purchased by Prescott Townsend, who had, in addition to his pedigreed family name, a Harvard education, ready cash.[42] The Barn was not short of patrons. Indeed, it was so popular that Elliot Paul, a Bohemian novelist and celebrity of the community, remarked that the management of the Schubert Theater in central Boston, in jealousy and desperation, had spread a rumor that the Barn Theater was a firetrap.[43]

Around the Barn sprang up a number of "tearooms," many of which served more than just tea. One of them, the Green Shutters, was opened on Cedar Lane Way, a street so difficult to find that even some longtime Hill residents were unaware of its existence. It had enough room for thirty patrons. Owner Billy Paul and his partner, Alan Wallace, discreetly handed out "heroic portions of gin and vermouth."[44] Other tearooms included

JOY STREET PLAYHOUSE

New England
Repertory Company

36 Joy Street

Playing Wednesdays Thru Saturdays

THE IMAGINARY INVALID, Moliere's gay farce
March 6, 11, 19, 21

OUR TOWN, a pulitzer prize winner by Thornton Wilder
March 4, 5, 12, 13, 20

ME AND HARRY, Charles Mergendahl's charming play
March 7

THE OLD LADIES, from Hugh Walpole's novel
March 14, 18

AS YOU LIKE IT, by Shakespeare
opens March 25 — playing all week

Reservations LAF. 4854   Curtain at 8:30

Poster for the Joy Street
Playhouse, 1920s. Courtesy
of the Beacon Hill Civic
Association.

March Hare on Myrtle Street, where the organizers served "meals and Tom Collinses." Saracen's Head was located on Joy Street, situated above the Barn (defying fire regulations). Other tearooms, some legitimate and some not, operated on Revere and Charles Streets. Outsiders, wrote Beebe, were sometimes introduced into the tumult and aesthetic delirium of the Beacon Hill scene. Many of them retired hastily, their wits and kidneys in a state of grievous disrepair, but a few apparently flourished, including several young faculty members and students from Harvard University.[45] On the North Slope lived also many boys and girls who might be married in the sight of God, explained the *Herald*, but had not applied for a license at City Hall.

Beacon Hill was not alone in hosting young Bohemians. In New York, Greenwich Village in lower Manhattan provided inexpensive tenements, circumvention of Prohibition laws, and the freedom to pursue lifestyles that were at odds with social conventions. In the Midwest, Chicago also offered the young Bohemians literary salons, living quarters, and the opportunities to pursue their various talents. Quite often these Bohemian centers reinforced each other by sending self-appointed "cultural ambassadors" from one to the other.

The Bohemian generation of the 1920s was markedly different from its predecessor. Instead of the optimism of Ralph Adams Cram's group, the revolt of the new Bohemians started with the disenchantment brought about by the war and changes in society. There was no presumed gentility in this generation, in comparison with the last. This generation wanted to break the constraints and boundaries in all forms of life and arts. Innocence had been lost, and America, to the Bohemians, had "come of age." Many residents of Beacon Hill watched the Bohemian colony with mixed feelings. Some were fascinated by it and experimented with the tearooms. Others worried over what it would do to the image of the Hill. The Joy Street Police Station installed two more night patrols. They raided parties from time to time, hoping to expose illegal operations only to be disappointed most of the time by what little they found. By the end of the 1920s, the artistic colony had run its course, however. The lost generation was either lost forever or matured into middle age, and this chapter of Bohemian life on the Hill was closed.

CHRISTMAS ON THE HILL

Among the many traditions of celebration in Boston, there is, perhaps, none more memorable or heralded than Christmas Eve on the Hill. People were writing about it in the 1920s. "There is a semireligious, semi-carnival spirit in the air that profoundly affects the observer and remains as a fragrant memory throughout the years," wrote one observer. Beacon Hill blossomed forth, he said, into a gorgeous mixture of light and color, music, and hospitality. "Boston has many sights and sounds that arouse the emotions and remain in the memory," he continued, "but the most soul-stirring and heart warming of all is Christmas Eve on Beacon Hill."[46]

Christmas Eve had not always carried these festive associations. In 1659 a Puritan law was passed in the Massachusetts Bay Colony to prohibit celebrations of Christmas. Whoever should be found observing any such day as Christmas or the like, said the law, "either by forbearing labor, feasting, or any other way upon such accounts as aforesaid, every such person so offending shall pay for every such offense five shillings, as a fine to the county." For almost two hundred years thereafter, the residents abstained from outward celebration. But that changed in 1856, when Christmas was proclaimed a legal holiday in the Commonwealth.

By the 1920s, Beacon Hill had developed its own special Christmas traditions. At dusk on Christmas Eve, described the *Transcript* on December 24, 1929, candles gleamed in the windows on Beacon Hill and avenues of light radiated "all the way to the suburbs."[47] And on this night these avenues would lead to the Hill, where, following custom, groups of singers would stroll from door to door singing traditional carols. The procession of singers would begin small and grow as it passed slowly from street to street, recalled another observer, "stopping at open houses of those who followed the ancient custom of welcoming the stranger in our midst. The hospitable doors would stand wide, with refreshments served from priceless heirlooms—wonderful old beaten silver, chaste in design and gleaming dully; lovely china and glass of odd and curious pattern; hand-made linen. To touch these was to touch hands across the centuries."[48]

There have been many explanations of the origin of the candle-lighting tradition on Beacon Hill. Feelings ran high when one version was considered more "official" than the other. Descendants of Mrs. Thomas Dwight argued that she, in 1870, was the first one to light candles on the windowsills of her home at 70 Beacon Street. Allen Chamberlain, after interviewing some old-timers in the neighborhood, believed that Alfred Shurtleff, a Unitarian clergyman, innocently started the tradition in 1893, when he was a boy living with his parents at 9 West Cedar Street. Alfred continued the practice the following year, catching the interest and curiosity of his neighbors. Candles appeared sporadically in other windows the following years. It was not until 1908 that a written invitation was sent around the Hill to make candle lighting a community event.

There were not many debates, however, about the origin of carol singing on the Hill. Early references to Christmas caroling date back to 1859, when the boys' choir from the Church of the Advent broke the still, cold night with their youthful voices. In the old tradition of the "waits," or village carolers, they traveled through the streets of Beacon Hill on Christmas Eve, muffled in cloaks and shawls and singing Christmas carols. The practice waned during the Civil War; it was many years until Mr. and Mrs. Ralph Adams Cram of 52 Chestnut Street revived it. One Christmas Eve, "it was, I think, in the year 1906," wrote Mr. Cram, "several friends were with us while I was trying vainly to brew mulled sack out of inapplicable materials, when my wife suddenly said, 'Let's go out and sing carols in the street!' With much timidity and deep misgivings, we sallied forth, although the night was cruel, and trembling attempted the Adeste Fideles beneath one or two windows of unconscious friends—then ran home again very frightened." The idea grew in the following years, and Mrs. Cram began a "regular campaign" to organize a band of carol singers.[49] As if to break the grip of the prohibitive law of earlier days, the Christmas idea quickly caught on and spread like wildfire. Soon it became a Beacon Hill institution.

At first the Crams gathered groups of children at their home to practice singing for Christmas Eve. Then Dr. Richard C. Cabot and his group of well-rehearsed singers started their procession at the Massachusetts General Hospital and toured the Hill, caroling as they marched through the streets with Paul Revere lanterns carried on poles to mark their progress.[50] Other groups of carolers would soon join them and music resounded from every

Christmas bell ringers, December 25, 1958. Courtesy of the *Herald-Traveler* and the Boston Public Library. Mrs. Arthur A. Shurcliff (*far left*), a prominent figure in Christmas celebration for many years, led this group at 66 Mount Vernon Street.

street on the Hill. Carols, laughter, and gaiety, described the local newspaper, carried it along from mansions ablaze with lights to tenements where one candle burned in a front window. Beacon Hill was the very capital of the Christmas spirit.

Together with candlelight and carolers came handbell ringing. Margaret Shurcliff, Marian Nichols's youngest sister, was considered its originator. Taught by her father, Dr. Arthur H. Nichols, himself an accomplished bell ringer, Margaret in turn passed on the family talent to her six children. In 1924 the family stood in the front yard of 55 Mount Vernon Street on Christmas Eve and gave their bell-ringing debut. "We only knew about six tunes so we rang these twice and moved on to another doorway," recalled Margaret. Apparently the Shurcliff performance was an instant success. "Flashes blinded us as cameras were snapped."[51]

As her children grew up, Margaret began to teach youngsters from the neighborhood. These pupils taught others, and so the New England Guild of Hand Bell Ringers came into being. Margaret Shurcliff was its president.

Each year, the bell ringers attracted thousands to the Hill and they followed the Shurcliff ringers, singing with them or just listening to the tone of the bells in the frosty air, reported the *Beacon Hill News*.[52]

According to different newspaper accounts, at least fifteen thousand people strolled the Hill on Christmas Eve of 1933. Until then, the visitors were generally attentive and almost "reverential." Things started to get out of hand by 1934. The behavior of the crowds that year, remarked Mark A. DeWolfe Howe to the editor of the *Transcript*, was more appropriate to the celebration of a football victory than to any recognition of the birth of Christ.[53] From there it went downhill. In 1935 the festivities were interrupted by roaring and hiccuping strangers, who drowned out carols with ribald songs, reported the *Transcript*.[54] A satiric poem was written by an anonymous resident describing the scene in 1936:

> When out on the street there arose such a clatter
> We sprang from our bed to see what was the matter,
> Away to the window we flew like a flash,

Boy bell ringers, December 25, 1952, photograph by Russ Adams of the *Herald-Traveler*. Courtesy of the Boston Public Library.

We pulled up the curtain and opened the sash.
The head lights of motors all parked in a row
Shed their beams over the asphalt like moon on the snow,
And down where the church steeple glowed in the sky,
A gang in a snake-dance, all yelling rushed by.
They whistled and shouted, called others by name
(To drown out the carols was clearly the game).
They were all by a spirit, in truth, stimulated,
But it wasn't the spirit St. Nick had created.
We pulled down the curtain and crept back to bed,
And as we sought slumber, my gentle mate said,
"I like Christmas Eve to be merry and bright,
But if that is the Spirit of Christmas,
Good night!"[55]

Efforts to temper the rowdy behavior, including those from the Beacon Hill Association, had no success. On December 20, 1937, the owners of Louisburg Square issued a warning that "Christmas Eve, let it be remembered, is not New Year's Eve." If the rowdiness persisted, the proprietors said, the observance would obviously have to be discontinued. Two days afterward, Dr. Richard C. Cabot announced that his carol band would not be performing again. For the first time in more than a quarter of a century, lamented the *Boston Herald*, Dr. Cabot and his band of carolers would be missing from Beacon Hill this Christmas Eve.[56] So ended a delightful epoch, at least temporarily.

Various explanations for the demise of the tradition have been discussed—from the effect of prolonged economic depression and the backlash against Prohibition to the coming of war in Europe. "America was still so young," wrote a resident to the *Transcript*, "and we had so few worthwhile customs to hand down to posterity. It seemed too bad to let such a custom be crushed by unthinking people."[57] Worthwhile customs, however, die hard on Beacon Hill. With the passing of time, those surrounding Christmas would reemerge. For now, the neighborhood, like the nation, awaited the onset of war.

CHAPTER THREE

War and Peace

1940–1950

There never was a good war or a bad peace.

BENJAMIN FRANKLIN
letter to Josiah Quincy
September 11, 1773

*I*N JUNE of 1939 the German consulate moved its office from State Street, in the heart of Boston's business district, to the residential heart of Beacon Hill. As the consulate staff began to set up shop at 39 Chestnut Street, the residents of Beacon Hill raised more than the proverbial eyebrow. They were not much comforted by the Germans' explanation that it was quite normal for an office to move from one place to another in a major city. One anxious resident, Susan Evans, wrote the Beacon Hill Association: "I consider the German Consulate a detriment to the street. I still own 28 Chestnut Street, and am interested in keeping the street on as high a level as is possible with the changing conditions." Emotions ran even deeper the following spring, when a swastika flag was unfurled at 39 Chestnut in observance of the fifty-first birthday of Adolf Hitler. The day the Third Reich's emblem was displayed, police and government agencies were swamped with phone calls from patriotic citizens asking why an American flag had not been unfurled alongside it. Officials at the Joy Street Police Station explained that there was no law preventing a foreign flag from being flown alone. Police were visibly nervous, however, about the explosiveness of the situation. The night passed in peace, and the police vigil relaxed when the swastika was removed the next day.

No less than the rest of America, Beacon Hill was growing exceedingly uneasy about German aggression in Europe as well as Japanese campaigns in Asia. American neutrality finally became an impossibility on Sunday, December 7, 1941, when at approximately 8:00 in the morning the imperial air force of Japan attacked Pearl Harbor—the day that would "live in infamy," as President Franklin D. Roosevelt told Congress the next morning. Within four hours of the president's address, America had declared war, and the country moved rapidly toward war readiness. Approximately thirty-one million Americans registered with draft boards, and about fifteen million of them eventually served in combat overseas. As resources were devoted to wartime production, a nation that had been struggling for years with economic depression and unemployment suddenly found itself hard-pressed to maintain essential institutions. The threat of enemy attacks on the American mainland seemed very real, even though combat was quite far from home. Civilian defense organizations were established throughout the country, with air raid wardens and civilian patrols in every neighborhood.[1]

OPPOSITE:
The war has ended, 1945. Courtesy of the Boston Public Library and the *Herald-Traveler*. Fred Apt sells the biggest news of the war on Tremont Street this morning.

81

Bomber heroes on parade, June 28, 1943. Courtesy of the *Herald-Traveler*. On their way to Boston Common, members of the crew of the *Memphis Belle* ride in army jeeps to the cheers of onlookers.

Beacon Hill, often a microcosm of dynamics in the nation at large, also redirected its energies toward war readiness and prepared for the worst. In March 1942 the gold dome of the State House, once dubbed "the hub of the solar system" by Oliver Wendell Holmes, Sr., was painted a dull war-gray so that the gleaming gold would not attract the attention of enemy aircraft.[2] Activities of the Beacon Hill Association were much curtailed, though, as John Codman wrote, the association was determined to keep intact and ready to function if the need arose.[3]

But in June 1943 the association decided that a neighborhood, even in time of world war, needed to remember its local responsibilities. Officers circulated a pamphlet reminding residents and businesses of their responsibilities to the Hill. "We can't call a special meeting, as many of you are too busy attending to the important job of winning the war," it began, "so we ask you to give five minutes to reading our suggestions and then to write us how you will help in our cooperative effort." There continued to be significant commercial value, the pamphlet explained, in the simple beauty of their Beacon Hill houses, shops, and streets. Even in wartime, visitors were coming from all over the United States to wander through the historic streets and browse the shops. People came, the association said, precisely because residents had maintained the spirit and tradition of old New England. "For our mutual protection, let's join in a pact to preserve the Colonial atmosphere of our Hill." The new pact involved putting up signs and other fixtures designed in keeping with the neighborhood's traditional architecture, while resisting the temptation to modernize inappropriately. The pact also involved a commitment to maintain the traditional exterior of buildings even when interior renovations were made. Beacon Hill's atmosphere, the pamphlet pointed

Air raid wardens, February 3, 1943. Courtesy of the Boston Public Library. Before graduating, Boston's first women wardens received final instruction on the use of the fire-pump extinguisher from Lt. Ethyl Clancy (*left*) of the MWDC, director of Training for the Boston Committee on Public Safety. The wardens are (*from left*) Lydia Evans, Jean Stowell Cullen, and Mrs. F. Van A. Wilmarth.

The State House dome, March 1942. Courtesy of the State Library of Massachusetts. The golden dome of the State House, once dubbed "the hub of the solar system" by Oliver Wendell Holmes, was painted a dull gray so that the gleaming gold would not serve as beacon to enemy aircraft.

out, had a fragile quality that "is at the mercy of us all." Beacon Hill must remain essentially Beacon Hill, come what may in the world beyond.

JAPANESE AND OTHER "STRANGERS"

*T*RY AS the association did, it was less than easy to maintain normalcy under wartime conditions—or even civility in some circumstances. Across America, distrust and hatred for Americans of Japanese descent were running high. At times, wild stories of sabotage circulated. In February 1942, under public pressure, President Roosevelt ordered the army to remove all persons of Japanese ancestry from the West Coast. Approximately 120,000 Japanese, two-thirds of them American citizens, were abruptly herded behind barbed wire and then shipped to relocation centers. Most of them lost their businesses and other possessions and were detained in prisonlike facilities. By the war's end, they found themselves without homes or means of livelihood.

During the peak of controversy several organizations, both religious and secular, launched major efforts to help these uprooted Americans relocate and find employment. Relocation hostels were opened up in New York, Pennsylvania, Washington, Illinois, Ohio, and other states to provide temporary lodging. In Boston an initiative was spearheaded by the Unitarian Service Committee and backed by a coalition of Christian denominations that included the Baptist Home Mission Society and the Congregational, Presbyterian, and Episcopal churches. Under the direction of the Reverend Edward A. Cahill, a native of Brockton, Massachusetts, and associate director of the Unitarian Service Committee, the effort established the first Relocation Hostel in New England at 6 Walnut Street, Beacon Hill. Some eighty Japanese-Americans were resettled. The efforts were sponsored by, among other groups, Labor's Educational Center, Inc., which owned 6 Walnut Street. The hostel would be entirely nonsectarian, explained the Reverend Cahill. There would be Buddhists, and, in fact, everything but Unitarians.

The Reverend Edward Cahill. Courtesy of the American Unitarian Association and the Andover-Harvard Theological Library. The associate director of the Unitarian Service Committee, the Reverend Cahill, together with a coalition of churches and private individuals, helped establish the first Japanese American relocation hostel, at 6 Walnut Street on Beacon Hill.

Not everyone on the Hill welcomed the resettlement initiative. "I have known several individual Japanese that I have liked," wrote one resident to John Codman, secretary of the Beacon Hill Association. "But very definitely I do not want a Japanese Relocation Hostel next door to me." Several reasons were listed, including potential negative impact on property values, sanitation, and security. "The selection of this location for the proposed hostel, so close to the Common, where so many U.S. service men congregate, seems unwise," argued the writer.[4]

In a letter to the Beacon Hill Association two days later, the same writer revealed his deeper objections. "If Boston is too easy," he said, "they will ship

Japanese Americans in the relocation hostel, 1945. Courtesy of the Unitarian Universalist Service Committee, Records, Andover-Harvard Theological Library of Harvard Divinity School. Japanese Americans, victims of the tragedy at home, were helped by the Unitarian Service Committee to find employment and relocate in Boston.

to Boston all the Japs from the Pacific Coast that they can. Obviously we do not want any of these Japs on Beacon Hill."[5] Faced with such sentiments, the Reverend Cahill tried to hold talks among representatives from both sides of the issue. He wanted opponents to understand that all the Japanese Americans in question had met security tests and were, in fact, loyal citizens. The coalition of sponsors, he said, was interested in seeing justice done "to this large group of our people who have been stigmatized because of ancestry." The debate finally shifted in favor of relocation on the Hill. But these deliberations held things up for more than a year, so that Beacon Hill's participation did not come into effect until several months before the atomic bomb officially brought Japan to its knees. At least for Cahill and his colleagues, the opening of 6 Walnut Street brought some measure of healing to an epidemic of national bitterness that even Beacon Hill could not avoid.

The problem of admitting Japanese was not the only issue of inclusiveness that dogged the association through the war years. The issue of membership recruitment raised its head now and again; it was a problem that had a long history. From 1925 to 1946, the association's membership grew by only 38, from 410 to 448, reflecting what some members suspected to be an unspoken tradition of restricting the influence of lower classes and nonwhite residents. It took a Quaker by the name of Margaret P. Welch to take the association to task over the matter. Welch was a resident in good standing of 20 Louisburg Square. On January 29, 1945, she boldly wrote to the association's president, Edward A. Taft: "Mr. Codman tells me that the Beacon Hill Association has no policy regarding the inclusion in its membership of the merchants on Charles Street and Cambridge Street, and I am writing to beg the Executive Committee to make it a definite policy to include as members *all* owners and tenants . . . and in the interest of the Association, as well as of our community, and of racial tolerance, we will do well to extend a welcoming hand and ask them to join us in a co-operative effort." The heretofore excluded groups to whom Welch alluded became more specific later in the letter. "I am confident that we shall fail in our purpose of maintaining our old traditions," she said, "until we sit down at the dinner table at annual and other meetings with the Jews and the Irish and the colored people, who are our neighbors, and make them feel that our Association is their Association, too."[6]

Apparently not all members felt so generous toward the merchants and North Slope neighbors as did Margaret Welch. Though no association member would ever openly advocate a policy of exclusiveness, subtle sentiments could sometimes be heard. Writing of the Margaret Welch initiative, a member told John Codman: "I think we are particularly fortunate in having so many new owners of the right sort on the Hill, and I would like to make sure that all of these are included in our members."[7]

RETURN OF THE GI

AFTER American victories abroad, Beacon Hill was swept by many of the same social dislocations that affected the nation. As multitudes of veterans came home, many were so deeply affected by the traumas and abnormalities of war that the "American dream" would not prove easy to grasp.

Demobilization of American military forces began as soon as the war ended. In April 1945 President Truman began the demobilization with the release of about seven million people from the army. After the Japanese surrender in August of that year, the pace accelerated, with a release each month, from October 1945 through February 1946, of no fewer than three-quarters of a million veterans. By June 1946 American ground, naval, and air forces had returned some 13 million veterans of World War II to civilian life.

Voices on Beacon Hill registered the uncertainties and angst over ominous housing and employment shortages. "Housing today has reached a low never before seen on the Hill or anywhere in America," reported the *Beacon Hill News* in October 1946. "Today hundreds of ex-GIs are homeless. Former war-workers are searching for homes to replace what they gave up when they heeded the call for help from our nation." The newspaper urged readers to pressure local politicians to support passage of a new housing bill. Governor Robert F. Bradford, for his part, encouraged the owners of large houses in places like Beacon Hill and the Back Bay to remodel them into small apartments and do their part to relieve the shortage. "There are many fine large houses in Beacon Hill and the Back Bay," said the governor, "which are empty or being used very little that could be remodeled to house a large number of ex-servicemen and their families, thus helping out the present emergency."[8]

Beacon Hillers were not particularly known for embracing calls for change from outsiders, the governor notwithstanding. As a longtime resident and real estate specialist, John Codman made it clear that remodeling was not likely to be an easy course. It might even be so costly, he warned, as to price the veteran out of the market, unless, he mused, the veteran in question was an admiral or had a rich wife.[9] Things were equally slow on the Hill when it came to creating employment. One veteran, the twenty-seven-year-old publisher of the *Beacon Hill News*, Raymond Bearse, wrote: "I have interviewed and talked with dozens of veterans and many of them encountered difficulty in getting started or to stay in business once they started."[10] Meanwhile, the prewar marriages of many veterans were proving untenable in the postwar period. One of every three ended in divorce. As public concern mounted, community organizations were roused to launch educational programs, trying to save the flagging family life of America. Without action, it was feared, democracy itself might be threatened.[11] If abroad Americans had made peace possible, it was not so at home in the lives of their own families.

One factor that complicated postwar adjustments was the fact that the country's psychological orientation to war still seemed to grip public consciousness. In the spring of 1947 one of the stranger events in Boston history occurred on the Boston Common, as the historic green was turned into a virtual peacetime army camp. An army band was playing one evening when crowds started to gather; children began running excitedly behind the band, and army units arrived to shore up the whole occasion. Looking on in disbelief was a veteran of foreign wars who had survived what he called "the blood-spattered hedgerows of Normandy" and the final march deep into the Third

Children and canon, 1946, photo by Leslie Jones. Courtesy of the Boston Public Library. Children pose on a captured German gun on Boston Common.

Reich. "This spring," he wrote anonymously in the *Beacon Hill News*, "swan boats and the ack-ack guns arrived simultaneously." It was a kind of "mass hypnosis," he said, reflecting what he considered a kind of "inherent militarism in Man." Only when people ceased tapping their feet to martial music and came to prefer a Strauss waltz, he wrote, might wars become a thing of the past.[12]

"What exactly is the miracle of war?" demanded another veteran, Allan Forbes, Jr., of 70 Beacon Street. Forbes was provoked by the euphoric tones of an article in the "Poetry Forum" of the *Beacon Hill News*, where a neighbor hailed the "miracle of war," praising the quiet courage and sacrifice of "insignificant boys who proved themselves heroes," and claimed that only in war were people able to see "the true magnificence of man." Allen Forbes fought back: "Does the Guernica depict a miracle? The 53 men who burned to death on a torpedoed tanker in less than three minutes during a winter night's storm in mid-Atlantic?" He went on: "Watching the flames pillaring high into the night but unable in any way to aid, I did not think it was a miracle. . . . The disemboweled youth that carpeted the long road from Normandie to the Elbe were not, to my way of thinking, miracles." In Forbes's view, the "quiet courage" was more a matter of resignation and self-preservation on the part of youth who wanted desperately to survive, with some pinch of duty thrown in. Should there be another war, concluded Forbes, "I relinquish to Miss Jackson my right to participation in it."[13]

The veterans who had once looked death in the eye came back with a heightened awareness of the world around them and refused to let sentiments of genteel insularity go unquestioned, least of all on America's original "Hill *genteel*." If GIs like Alan Forbes could never be the same, neither could the communities they had long called home. Time would be needed for normalcy to be redefined.

THE BRICK SAVERS RIDE AGAIN

R ESIDENTS of West Cedar Street were awakened one spring morning in 1947 by commotion under their windows. Looking out, they found work crews tearing up their redbrick sidewalks with picks and shovels, planning to replace the bricks with cement. Enraged, many ran out of their houses trying to stop the workmen. Some housewives, children, and grandmothers tried tactics of nonviolent resistance, bringing chairs and rugs to sit down and "guard their time-honored bricks from vandalism."[14] A woman by the name of Mrs. George Smith got down on her hands and knees and began replacing in her sidewalk all the dislocated bricks she could find. A sympathetic milkman lay across the remaining bricks and said to Mrs. Smith, "I am on your side."[15]

The city's action, a resident of West Cedar Street later commented, "was not only an insult in view of the petition of 300 residents, requesting that the bricks be kept, but injury because, since the street had already been torn up, residents now had no place to walk."[16] The *Boston Herald* warned in an editorial that the "sound wave zooming into Beacon Street is no traffic roar or hurricane. It is the rising protest of Beacon Hillites. Mr. Curley had better beware."[17] With the mayor now openly named and blamed, Beacon Hill's Second Battle of the Bricks had officially begun.

Since the First Battle of the Bricks twenty-seven years before, there had been several other skirmishes with the city over the cherished bricks. Each time the neighborhood won. The street commissioners, however, kept coming back. Visitors to Beacon Hill, said the *Boston Herald*, often complained about the uneven brick sidewalks on this most famous slope. Hill residents, however, "have become as nimble as antelopes with the years and hardly ever notice the imperfections under their feet. But take those away, and there'd be trouble."[18] The city warned of the potential costs of having to pay damages to persons suing over injury caused by the bricks and won sympathy from some Hill residents.[19] But the majority of Beacon Hillers loved their bricks and wanted them to stay.

On April 29, 1947, the women of West Cedar Street planned another sit-down strike to prevent, as the *Post* described it, "the construction of a grano-

Battle of the Bricks, 1947. Courtesy of the *Beacon Hill News*. A group of Beacon Hill residents staged a sit-down demonstration to protest the city's removal of their beloved redbrick sidewalk.

lithic sidewalk in place of the traditional red bricks over which generations of Beacon Hill residents have trod and tripped."[20] West Cedar Street, according to an article in the *Boston Herald*, looked like something the army left behind in France. A small group of women sunned themselves on the sidewalk and quietly stated that when the workmen crossed Revere Street they were going to move into action. As the watchful women chatted among themselves on the sidewalk, two workmen with picks on their shoulders suddenly appeared and began digging up the bricks on the opposite side of the street. Immediately, the women moved their chairs across the street, and reinforcements of both women and men poured out of historic houses on both West Cedar and Pinckney Streets to join the "dignified resistance."[21]

On April 30 Mayor Curley entered his office in downtown Boston only to find himself faced with seventy-five Hillers who were well prepared to defend their beloved brick sidewalks. The ever-vigilant man of real estate, John Codman, explained that Hillers paid the city more in taxes than the Hill received in services; so it would be only right for the city to do well by the Hill in this instance. Pushing a "technical argument," the architect Dana Somes insisted that concrete actually had little advantage over brick, winter or summer. Trying to pull the mayor's heartstrings over matters sentimental and aesthetic, Margaret Welch reminded him that Beacon Hill antiquities were a national attraction. Cement, she said, "is as inappropriate on Beacon Hill as elevators in St. Kevin's Cave in Limerick." Williamsburg, she added, was a mere reproduction. "We, on Beacon Hill inherited the original, and we had the obligation to pass it on intact to coming generations."[22]

Mr. Curley, no stranger to reading the political winds, decided it was time to bow to those he'd come to call the "royal purple." In view of the tide of citizens sweeping down from Beacon Hill, he said, "I don't think the Public Works Commissioner is justified in taking a position like that of Dame Partington, who tried to sweep the ocean back with a broom." Echoing the rhetoric of the protestors, Curley told his intense audience, "Beacon Hill is in the same category as Williamsburg. People from all over the world go to see the restoration there. It is known for its historical, sentimental and aesthetic values. I think that's true of Beacon Hill also, and the hill is not a restoration— it's real."[23] The "tide" gave him two minutes of applause while the mayor beamed at news cameras. Triumphantly, the "ocean" receded on its own.

Make the sidewalk shine for Easter, March 26, 1948. Courtesy of the *Boston Herald.* "Mrs. F. Gordon Patterson, who last year saved the brick sidewalks from being replaced, directed the work today, helped by Deborah and Jimmy Parkman."

The unfolding of this drama was attracting more than local interest, according to commentary in the *Beacon Hill News.* A group of private citizens, battling in the face of what appeared overwhelming odds, had scored a major victory. Apparently, however, it was an assessment shared well beyond the camp of the winning party. Letters of support poured in from all over the country. Wrote Minnie Jensen of New York: "My husband and I are so glad you will not allow them to destroy those beautiful old streets. We stop each year on our way back from Maine at the Bellevue Hotel in Boston, and we just love to walk up and down those beautiful old streets and admire your beautiful old homes on Beacon Hill."[24] Another writer observed that in an age of wars, there were few bloodless victories like the Battle of the Bricks. So rousing was the acclaim that Francis W. Hatch, an author, poet, and composer, leaped into action, creating the now famous song entitled "God Save the Bricks on Beacon Hill":

> God save the bricks on Beacon Hill, Hallelujah
> Those walks we love so well on Beacon Hill
> The vandals who'd replace 'em, we'll drive right out of town
> You can't down the folks on Beacon Hill.

> So that is our position, we hope we've made it clear
> We'll fight you by petition, day by day and year by year.

> Keep modern hands from Beacon Hill, Hallelujah
> Drive them out like termites from the sill
> Our battlefield of Bulfinch we'll fight for to the grave
> Oh God save the soul of Beacon Hill, we implore you—
> God save the whole of Beacon Hill.[25]

MOTHERS AGAINST STORROW DRIVE

NOT ALL the evils facing postwar Boston were legacies of war. For decades the city had been wrestling with mounting problems brought about by the automobile. By the late 1940s, Boston was considered one of the worst traffic areas in the country, with nearly half the streets virtually blocked by parked cars and the average driving speed falling to 8.5 miles an hour. Traffic congestion was causing economic losses to seaports, the airport, and to other businesses. For years the state and city legislature and the Metropolitan District Commission (MDC) wrestled with the daunting problem. One solution, strongly supported by Governor Dever in 1946, started a public uproar on Beacon Hill.

Designed by the MDC, this solution called for a new parkway to be constructed to allow traffic a route west out of the city. The proposed six-lane highway would run from Charles Street through the Storrow Memorial Embankment along the Charles River to Soldiers Field Road on the western outskirts of the metropolitan area. Construction would strip seventy feet of land from the embankment, including one of the two million square feet in the Esplanade, and come within 110 feet of the Hatch Memorial Shell. The cost was initially estimated at six million dollars. Such a parkway, claimed the MDC commissioner, was a most important factor in the elimination of traffic congestion in downtown Boston.[26]

As soon as the proposal was announced, a public outcry went up in the neighborhoods of Beacon Hill, Back Bay, and the West End. Some claimed that to build a highway across the heart of the parkland violated the fundamental principle of the philanthropist James Jackson Storrow.[27] In 1903 Storrow had worked tirelessly to get the legislature to dam up the sides of the Charles River, which would transform its surrounding lands from mud flats into a park. Later his widow had donated one million dollars to the Commonwealth in memory of her husband and made the park a reality. For her generosity, the state named the park Storrow Memorial Embankment. To construct a highway through the park would destroy the "restful, suburban-like quiet so amazing here in the midst of the noisy city."[28]

In essence residents of areas surrounding the embankment, or the Esplanade, as it was known, had grown to love it for its natural beauty. Arthur Fiedler, director of the Boston Pops Orchestra and conductor of a renowned concert series along the Esplanade, publicly joined the opposition in the summer of 1946. "It would be a shame," he said, "to have a six-lane highway through the esplanade, especially so near the shell where we give our concerts." Claiming that he was opposed to the highway from an aesthetic point of view, Mr. Fiedler called himself a "fan" of the Esplanade. While living in downtown Boston, he walked at least four miles daily along the Esplanade for exercise and contemplation.[29] Personages like Fiedler were joined by many others in the area, from Blair Gamble, a retired employee of Massachusetts General Hospital and resident of Grove Street who loved his daily stroll through the park, to Inda Kaufman of Newbury Street, who saw the Esplanade as a peaceful and beautiful place that should be left alone.

As forces against the highway grew, some groups launched studies to show that the highway would not really ease the traffic bottleneck in downtown Boston. One such group, comprising concerned citizens from Beacon Hill and the surrounding communities, took the name "Storrow Memorial Embankment Protective Association," and called on its thousand members to protest passage of the highway bill at the State House.[30] Other opponents challenged the legal right of the city to build a highway on public land.[31] Eventually, no fewer than thirty civic groups and several thousand residents of the West, South, and North Ends of Boston, in addition to those from Beacon Hill and Back Bay, signed the "Save the Esplanade" petitions addressed to Governor Dever as part of the community-based drive against the highway.

But perhaps the most dogged fighting force behind the resistance emerged among a passionate group of Beacon Hill and Back Bay residents—mothers of the fledgling baby boom generation. "I used to take Tim out on the Esplanade," recalled Rosemary Whiting of Brimmer Street, a war bride from England who settled on Beacon Hill after World War II with her physician husband. "It was at the time one of the few long, uninterrupted city riverside parks that had greenery all the way and no traffic." What Rosemary did daily to "escape the city" was to walk with her baby carriage on the Esplanade and then sit on the grass while her son, Tim, played in the playground.[32] Many mothers from the low-income residential blocks of the West End also shared Rosemary's experience. To them and their children, the Charles River Basin, with its restful river park, baseball diamond, community garden, and tennis courts, was a place of beauty available to all—very much in the spirit of James Storrow. A highway, to these mothers, would replace the restful greenery with gassy, grinding automobiles.

When Beacon Hill residents Rosemary Whiting and Elizabeth Forbes discovered that West End residents were planning to send a group to the State House that included some mothers and babies, they took their own baby carriages out to the streets and stopped every mother with a baby on Charles Street, rousing passionate concerns about the looming prospect of losing the playgrounds and walk zones. "If we gave you notice," they asked each mother, "would you bring your babies and come to the State House with us and say we don't want to have this road?" The response was overwhelming. Planning moved ahead spontaneously, complete with volunteers making signs for a march on the State House.

On March 2, 1949, the mothers of Boston set out for the State House, seeking their day before the governor's staff. As Rosemary Whiting and Elizabeth Forbes walked up Beacon Street, they were excited to find mothers with babies pouring out of the side streets to join the march, some with banners saying, "We don't want the Esplanade Road" and "What about our playground?" By the time the mothers joined other protestors at the State House, the delegation was so large that the hearing had to be moved to a larger hall. During the course of the hearing, about twenty mothers decided to try to see the governor in person, only to be told he was too busy to see them. "We're just going to stay here and wait," said the determined mothers. The door finally opened to Governor Dever's office and in went the mothers and the babies—many of the babies were now cranky and wailing, and the older kids strewed cookie crumbs all over the place. Mary Thornton of the West End directly approached the governor's desk. Pregnant with her second child and holding her two-year-old by the hand, she told Governor Dever of a letter she had received from city government before she had moved to Boston. The letter promised that she would be bringing her children into a city where everyone had the best possible chance to live a happy, productive life. "And now you are going to take my children's playground away from them?" she asked. Dever assured her that one of his staff would be contacting the mothers over the issue.[33]

The media relished the "Mothers against Storrow Drive" story. The next day, headlines in the *Christian Science Monitor* heralded the convergence of hundreds of women and children on the State House protesting the multi-million-dollar highway bill. A tug-of-war ensued between the governor's office, the city, and the MDC on the one hand, and the coalition of opponents on the other. A compromise bill was finally reached. "If everybody will just keep his shirt on," claimed an editorial in the *Boston Traveler*, "we think a perfectly palatable solution can be worked out."[34] The compromise bill recommended filling in an equivalent portion of the Charles River Basin for all the parkland taken for the highway. Recreational areas would also be restored and improved. Moreover, the parkway would be depressed from Clarendon Street to Massachusetts Avenue with four lanes instead of six, and overpasses would be built at intervals for pedestrians.

Governor Dever's aides proceeded to "ram" the parkway bill through the house, as the *Christian Science Monitor* reported it.[35] An eight-million-dollar bond, as part of the hundred-million-dollar bond to be issued by the legislature, was released to finance the construction. Calling it "a happy ending of a rugged fight," the governor signed the Embankment Bill on May 6, 1949. Dever personally made it a point to be on hand for the ribbon cutting that marked the opening of the highway on June 14, 1951. Even though the highway represented a loss to the fighting mothers, many believed they had at least moved the politicians toward a more acceptable outcome. "When I walk along the esplanade I pass the children's playground," reflected Rosemary Whiting in her autobiography. "It makes me feel happy to think what, in a rather humbling way, we helped to build."[36]

NOWHERE TO GO BUT DOWN

THE FIGHT against Storrow Drive, as residents of Beacon Hill soon realized, was only the first in a series of battles against encroachments of the modern age. By mid-century, increased federal aid for urban improvements gave Boston the hope of launching an all-out attack on traffic snarls. The goal of the Boston Public Works Commission, said its commissioner, William Callahan, was to iron out the wrinkles in its postwar highway pattern.[37] The designs of Callahan, later famous for lending his name to one of Boston's main underwater tunnels, were just one part of a series of public works initiatives across the city.[38] Among these initiatives was the construction of a garage below the Common, which Beacon Hill residents and many others considered sacred ground.

Back in 1634 Beacon Hill's legendary "first resident," William Blackstone, had conveyed forty-eight acres of land to the fledgling Boston community. The town, in turn, set aside that land, in good English tradition, as "commonage," or common land shared by the general public. Thus originated America's oldest park. Since then, the Boston Common had seen formative national events, including the mustering of an army by George Washington, the stationing of British Redcoats, and the training of Union soldiers during the Civil War. It had also witnessed some of the more ignominious events, such as the beheading of the Quaker martyr Mary Dyer. During colonial days the Common had sustained the community by providing fodder for its herds, and, in latter days, it had also enhanced leisure, as the Frog Pond in winter supported long hours of skating pleasure. To many Beacon Hill residents, the Common was, like the Esplanade, an oasis and an emerald expanse amid the close quarters of city living. It was not something to spoil with a garage.

The idea of an underground garage was, in fact, an old idea being revisited. In the earliest proposal, dating back to 1928, planners had envisioned twenty thousand cars under the Common. In the 1940s the legislature approved the construction of a garage for approximately thirty-five hundred cars. But World War II and the shortage of steel after the Korean War intervened to scuttle the effort. Now a new vision would not just open a massive space for parking, but make parking a *business* that was financially viable. The plan involved having the Foundation Company, a New York construction company, raise eleven million dollars for construction of the garage, operate it as a private company for forty years, and then give the garage back to Boston. The city, in the meantime, would receive 2 percent of the operating proceeds annually as a rental fee. The idea gained rapid support from both city and state governments. Mayor John Hynes appealed to President Truman for the necessary allocation of steel. Governor Foster Furcolo established the Massachusetts Parking Authority and empowered it to undertake the project.

Many of Boston's citizenry disagreed with the governor and the mayor. And there ensued a ten-year battle between the mayor and his men on the one hand, and a variety of opponents with an array of charges and concerns on the other. The opponents' concerns ranged from the potential for disfiguring the beauty of the Common[39] and ruining a historical treasure,[40] to possible violation of the Parkman Trust, which was dedicated to improving the Common.[41] Many individuals and organizations charged the city with empowering a for-profit group to run a public facility under tax-exempt status, and emphasized the potential for cronyism and giving of special favors to friends of the legislature.[42]

Despite massive efforts by community organizations and individuals to stop the project, Commissioner Callahan's dream of building an underground garage in Boston's historic center went forward. Neighbors still succeeded, however, in ensuring that the construction remained hidden from sight and kept a vigilant eye on business operations. They eventually struck back full force when it was revealed that corruption was infusing the whole operation. As John Codman had predicted in the early days, the construction of the underground garage opened a door to the "most incredibly involved case of grand larceny" in the history of the Commonwealth.[43] This

Putting the lid on, August 16, 1961. Courtesy of the *Boston Herald*. Construction workers put finishing touches on the rooftop area of the Boston Common Garage.

included the subterfuge of fake engineering, legal, and finder's fees, the wholesale falsification of official records, and the establishment of a fictitious corporation in order to receive kickbacks amounting to approximately eight hundred thousand dollars. A yearlong investigation and the trial that ensued led to the conviction of, among others, a judiciary court judge, several lawyers, engineers, and the chairman of the Massachusetts Parking Authority. The Common Garage scandal became such a landmark case in the legal history of the state that it led to the creation of the Massachusetts Crime Commission. A conflict-of-interest law was passed to prevent such abuse of public funds and trust from happening again. Throughout the "purification process," a key prosecutor of the case was a Beacon Hill native and former president of the Beacon Hill Association—Gael Mahony.

Prosecutors of the Common Garage scandal, 1963, photograph by Frank Kelly for the *Herald-Traveler.* Courtesy of the Boston Public Library. *(From left)* Gael Mahony, Attorney General Edward Brooke, Walter Skinner, and William Dockser.

WEST END STORY

By mid-century the West End of Boston, Beacon Hill's neighboring community, had become a vibrant potpourri of ethnic groups. "On a Sunday just in my apartment building," remembered one West Ender, "the smell of all different nations filled the hallways with the aromas of their ethnic cooking. We had Irish, Jewish, Italians, Yankees, Greeks, and Ukrainians."[44] Only a half-century before, the West End had been known as a transient stop for immigrants before they moved on to better places. Since then the neighborhood had quietly evolved into a stable community when many groups decided to stay and call it home. By the 1940s many residents had lived there among families and friends for more than a generation, and to some the West End was the only community they knew. By the end of World War II, the West End had become extremely diverse, claiming more than twenty different types of ethnic background. And while ethnic solidarity was affirmed, this diverse population had also found a way to weave its diversity into a common fabric of community life.

Unfortunately, not all onlookers deemed the community situation so viable. Mayor John Hynes and the Boston Housing Authority, for example, considered the area "substandard," and, therefore, a perfect candidate for clearance, aided by federal dollars for urban renewal. The mayor officially launched his "West End Project" on April 11, 1953, hoping to relocate some 2,248 families from the West End to other parts of Boston. No fewer than 682 of the 739 residential buildings would be demolished in order to make way for new construction. City inspectors, for their part, estimated that 80 percent of the housing structures in the West End were "below standard," 60 percent of them rat infested, and 80 percent with no outside fire escapes.

For many of those who actually lived in the West End, however, the neighborhood did not feel quite so "substandard." Like its neighbor Beacon Hill, the area had a history of development and evolution that carried some considerable pride and a history that reached back to colonial days. From its earliest times the West End, or New Field as it was called, provided verdant pastureland and orchards.[45] The value of the land dropped with the opening of one of Boston's fourteen so-called "rope walk industries," but rebounded in the late eighteenth century with the opening of the West Boston Bridge, now the Longfellow Bridge, which links Boston with Cambridge. By 1820 the West End competed with Beacon Hill for well-to-do residents.

There was, perhaps, an inevitable shift in the 1840s with the rapid rise of industrialization and the rising popularity of the horse-drawn "omnibus." It was then that migrant labor began to arrive in large numbers from out-lying rural areas, attracted by new jobs in the city. The shift was further re-inforced by the arrival of Irish immigrants escaping the potato famine of 1846. There followed a succession of immigrants: European Jews who were escaping the pogroms in Russia, and then other immigrants from Italy, Poland, Albania, and Lithuania. As more and more single-family homes were converted into rental apartments, upper- to middle-class families re-treated to the suburbs, facilitated by the horse-drawn omnibuses on Cam-bridge Street. By the late 1850s, the West End had become primarily a diverse working-class community.

The feasibility of some kind of surgical removal of "urban blight" in the West End was made even more questionable by links that had grown over many years between West End neighborhoods and those of Beacon Hill. In fact, throughout the nineteenth century it was not clear to most area resi-dents where the North Slope of Beacon Hill ended and the West End of Boston began. The African Meeting House on Joy Street, for instance, served the black population living both in the West End and on the North Slope of Beacon Hill. Vilna Shul, the only synagogue that was built to serve the Jewish population in the West End, was located on the Hill's Phillips Street in 1919. Many Beacon Hill philanthropists also chose the West End as their beneficiary. Joseph Lee, a prominent Beacon Hiller whose father was credited with founding the public playground movement, remained a strong supporter of the West End. Elizabeth Peabody, who started one of the first kindergartens on Beacon Hill, also moved her social experiment into the West End by establishing the Elizabeth Peabody Settlement House, which provided social and educational assistance to generations of immigrants.

Still, by the 1950s much housing in the West End had surely deteriorated, with once-spacious mansions and gardens replaced by cramped boarding-houses, built with little consideration for open space or building regulations.

It was not totally without logic that Mayor Hynes classified the West End, together with other areas such as Roxbury, Jamaica Plain, Charlestown, and Dorchester, as "obsolete neighborhoods." The West End Project was one piece in the larger postwar strategy for slums. Hynes was thinking in grand terms of dealing an "all-out blow against the accumulative slums of the last 100 years."[46] The city estimated that forty million dollars would be spent, with Boston riding the wave of two federal housing acts targeting blighted cities throughout America.[47]

In the 1950s public confidence in the federal government was high. The nation had recently emerged from the New Deal and World War II, and the government was considered a benevolent force that could be relied upon to do the right thing. Most Bostonians and institutions supported the slum clearance initiative, and Mayor Hynes hailed urban renewal as "the salvation of old cities like Boston."[48] In urban renewal there might be an impetus for the local economy, many felt, with private enterprises willing to invest in the rejuvenated cities.[49] There were also the doubters uttering grim jeremiads. Gabriel F. Piemonte, an attorney who maintained an office in the neighboring North End, insisted that "the history of the West End Project will haunt the housing administration to eternity."[50] Joseph Lee echoed with this satire: "Blasted be the poor, for theirs is the kingdom of nothing, and blasted be the meek, for they shall be kicked off the earth."[51]

Bucking residential opposition, the city, through its newly formed Boston Redevelopment Authority, decided to move forward with operations. On April 25, 1958, the residents of the West End received registered letters from City Hall informing them that the BRA had taken over their property by eminent domain in order to eliminate a substandard residential area. Even though they had previously heard promises that low-rent housing alternatives would be available, no such provision was included in the eviction notices distributed in 1958. Soon the federal bulldozers moved in, razing buildings that had been abandoned by their former occupants. It was like "a dragon waiting to eat the old house shells as soon as their occupants move out."[52] By the late 1950s the West End looked like a bombed-out wasteland. For close to a decade after that, the area was called the "biggest parking lot in Boston."[53]

The impact on individuals was devastating. Uprooted from their close-knit community, they were scattered far and near, "from Alaska to Italy."[54] Having little money and fewer choices, most of them searched desperately for accommodations, some moving to other working-class neighborhoods. The abrupt change brought about by the relocation put the stability, health, and well-being of many West Enders in jeopardy. Even several years after relocation, 72 percent of the women and 66 percent of the men who had moved wanted to go back. In interviews many of them revealed shared sentiments: "Something of me went with the West End"; "I felt as though I lost everything."[55] Against the backdrop of these social dislocations, West End renovation was awarded to Charles River Park, Inc., which decided to build high-rise apartments primarily for middle- to upper-income individuals. Many saw it as a case of Robin Hood in reverse, "taking houses from the poor to provide housing for the rich."[56]

Beacon Hill residents looked on with concern. Though many supported urban renewal in theory, what was happening in the West End forced them to reexamine the validity of the city's approach. Outcry over the human cost of the West End Project triggered much rethinking and many public debates. The mood of the country about bulldozer-oriented urban renewal was also shifting in favor of more moderate rehabilitation. As the Civil Rights Movement gained momentum in the 1960s, ethnic community groups assumed greater involvement in the renewal process. The West End experience served, in its own sad way, as a major turning point in Boston. As the horrors of the West End story spread, resistance grew in other neighborhoods earmarked for destruction. Many were subsequently saved from a similar fate.[57]

A HILL FOR HISTORY

*F*OR SOME years the experience of the West End sent shivers through Beacon Hill. Many residents wondered if the Hill could be subject to similar external tampering from government. Social engineering from the outside had never gone down well with Hillers, and once again their own historical heritage seemed in need of watchful protection. In the spring of

1953 an article by William Kinney in *National Geographic* caught the eye of John Codman. It explained how the residents of Georgetown had managed to get Congress to recognize their neighborhood as a historic district. Recognizing the obvious similarities between Georgetown and Beacon Hill, Codman was propelled into action. On April 14, 1953, he sent a letter to Kinney asking for more information. This was the beginning of a long correspondence between Codman and representatives of other historic neighborhoods in an effort to save the Hill for posterity.

As Codman soon learned, initiatives for historic-district preservation in America had been going on for quite some time. In 1931 the city of Charleston, South Carolina, was designated an "old and historic district" by enactment of a local ordinance. In 1937 the French Quarter of New Orleans was similarly protected through an amendment to the Louisiana Constitution. The start of World War II put a temporary stop to such initiatives, but they revived soon after the war. In 1946 Alexandria, Virginia, passed an ordinance, followed in 1947 by Winston-Salem, North Carolina. By 1953 eight old neighborhoods had achieved Historic District status. Under the law of Historic Districts, no changes were allowed to exterior architectural features of buildings without the permission of the respective architectural commissions. Through architectural control, as Codman and the Beacon Hill Association concluded, a neighborhood with valued historical roots could be deliberately and permanently protected from becoming a slum.

The association was, by now, a mature neighborhood organization with decades of public campaign experience. Drawing on that expertise, Codman and his associates embarked on a new crusade to designate the Hill a Historic District. A survey was made of the Hill. The result was two large-scale maps marking the architectural style of buildings and the current use of each structure.[58] The association filed a bill with the state legislature in January 1955, asking that the South Slope be designated a Historic District. Selecting only the South Slope was a strategic decision, since many believed that including the North Slope and the Flat in the same bill could increase resistance and controversy and make the bill's passage impossible.

The association's campaign gained extensive media coverage—the largest ever on behalf of Beacon Hill.[59] By June 23, less than six months into the crusade, more than eleven thousand lines of newspaper print had been published in favor of the effort. Newspaper clippings reveal that stories were carried by newspapers of many states, including Kentucky, Michigan, Louisiana, Florida, Alabama, New York, and Pennsylvania. "Certain public-spirited citizens had now petitioned the legislature to set aside, as an historical area, this special section on Beacon Hill that comprises roughly the land bought by the Mt. Vernon proprietors in 1795," reported the Catholic Archdiocese's Boston newspaper, the *Pilot*.[60] "Something solid in its architectural simplicity promises to endure for centuries if only given the chance to do so," reported the *Christian Science Monitor*.[61]

In explaining what was at stake in the Beacon Hill situation, journalists took some pains to show the price of losing historical landmarks. Many a priceless landmark was gone, observed the *Christian Science Monitor*, a tragic example being the failure of Boston's General Court (by only a single vote) to save the John Hancock house. The survival of Beacon Hill as a monument to American history up to the middle of the twentieth century was more a matter of chance than of planning, noted the *Boston Herald*: "It is being chipped away even now. Boston and the Commonwealth owe it to themselves to provide adequate protection for the area." Editorials in the *Boston Daily Record* argued that Beacon Hill could reasonably be called a shrine "in which the present bows reverently to the past."[62] Destroying Beacon Hill, its writers argued, would be almost as much of a sacrilege as dismantling the White House. "A hundred years before," the paper concluded, "we tore down John Hancock's beautiful home near the State Capitol and have regretted the act ever since."[63]

With the media stirring public passions, Beacon Hill's request for legislative protection took on a certain urgency at the State House, and pressure mounted for passage of the legislation. The association complemented the media crusade with grassroots outreach in the community by staging public forums and distributing pamphlets. Helen Duprey Bullock of the National Trust for Historic Preservation was invited to speak on the subject in January 1955. The occasion was used not only to inform attendees about the issues, but also to mobilize their support for the new bill. When it came time for the Massachusetts Senate to review the legislation, more than five hundred Beacon Hill supporters crowded into the hearing room. In addition, nineteen public and private groups went on record in favor of the association's initiative, led by Mayor Hynes, with another seven state representatives and one senator also expressing their support. "If anything goes wrong with the current movement to formally make Beacon Hill a historical area and preserve its living essence for all time," wrote a Beacon Hill resident, Rudolph Elie, "I shall renounce Boston forever and move to San Francisco."[64]

Elie did not have to move to San Francisco. On July 28, 1955, Senate Bill 605 passed the legislature and was signed into law by Governor Christian Herter, thus creating the Beacon Hill Historic District. Also created was the Beacon Hill Architectural Commission, a watchdog for the district. Newspapers appeared exultant with the result. The *Boston Daily Globe* exclaimed that the Hill had saved the Hill, working in the spirit of Bulfinch, the Mount Vernon Proprietors, and the greats of old; also at work were the vigilance of their successors in the modern Beacon Hill Association and the tearful tragedies of neighborhoods like the West End.

Winning the legal battle to preserve the Hill represented only the first step, pointed out Gael M. Mahony, the twenty-nine-year-old president of the Beacon Hill Civic Association[65] and a new assistant U.S. attorney. Invoking the words of the first governor, John Winthrop, he called upon Hillers to set an example that would reach beyond its own back step. "The eyes of the public are upon us," he said. "Let us all see to it that the Hill is not just the oldest district still intact in Boston, but the most progressive. Let us maintain our property and keep our sidewalks, streets and alleys clean. We should set an example to the whole of the City."[66] Mahoney's was a large vision for a small hill. But perhaps this particular hill, of all in America, deserved to think historically large.

CHAPTER FOUR

Reinventing Beacon Hill
1960–2000

Quality that's all its own
This little village overgrown—
A courteous grace one only meets
On Beacon Hill in little streets.

MINA DEHART MIDDLETON

As the 1960s arrived, historic Boston was sliding into a period of unseemly urban blight. The city built on a hill "for all to see" appeared to have become, as one observer put it, "an over-ripe plum permitted to shrink in the midst of great opportunities."[1] Past visions of urban renewal seemed to have lost their champions. Jungles of decayed housing spread across the city's storied neighborhoods, encroaching Bunker Hill, surrounding Faneuil Hall, and engulfing the Old North Church.[2] Nearly three-quarters of all buildings in central Boston had been built as far back as the Civil War and World War I, and most of those were in disrepair. Broken and boarded windows, sagging doors, peeling paint, and trash were familiar sights.

The fact that Boston's property tax was the highest among American cities—two and a half times New York's or Chicago's, three times Philadelphia's, and three and a half times Cleveland's—did not help. In fact, it had created a vicious cycle. *Fortune* called it a "poisoning well" for real estate investors, "keeping the postwar U.S. building boom at bay."[3] The absence of new construction eroded the tax base, which only led to more tax increases. Traditional industries, such as textiles, leather, and shoe making, had gradually left Boston, and new industries were not moving in.

Meanwhile, the city's population was also in serious decline. Between 1950 and 1960 it had decreased by 15.4 percent, the third largest drop among America's two hundred largest cities.[4] One of every four citizens had moved elsewhere, at an astonishing rate of twenty thousand a year, only partially offset by new births and immigrants.[5] In the face of these demographics, and the state of the city more generally, the cradle of liberty was fast becoming what the *Economist* called "a graveyard of hopes."[6]

AWAKENINGS

In various neighborhoods, including Beacon Hill, a new consciousness was stirring about the extent to which Boston lagged behind other cities in urban development. Perhaps the experience of the West End's "renewal" had frightened and discouraged some inner-city neighborhoods, not to mention the politicians, from moving programs ahead more vigorously. In the

Property owner's protest, January 7, 1962. Courtesy of the *Boston Herald*. Dorothy Clark surveys trash and garbage strewn in the alley behind Temple Street, following the morning trash collection by the city. She and other residents of Beacon Hill planned to make a formal protest to city health officials if no action was taken.

West End had arisen Charles River Park: "banal groupings of blunt, balconied towers on a treeless plain."[7] Beacon Hill barely escaped the revitalizing bulldozers, even though its South Slope was protected as a Historic District. But the notion that *all* urban renewal should cease was not viable either. Neighborhoods like the North Slope of Beacon Hill were deteriorating at an alarming speed. Members of the Civic Association began carefully to analyze the forces producing these effects. President Gael Mahony concluded that the leading cause may have been overcoverage of land due to lack of zoning and proper building laws. "We are paying dearly now," he said, "for our past sins of neglect of proper planning."[8]

Leaders on Beacon Hill, as well as in the city at large, called for some serious soul-searching about Boston's future in the hope of countering fears that investors and visionaries would flee, like many of the middle class, to the suburbs. One city planner, Maurice Rolivar, was not about to give up on Boston. The city, he said, "is located in the right place, and it has a 'soul'—an individual character."[9] Mayor John F. Collins began to thrust the issue of urban redevelopment center stage, appointing a new Director of Development, the first in Boston's history. The new development czar, Edward T. Logue, was a young lawyer who had gained national attention through assisting New Haven's mayor in directing that city's urban renewal. After settling down at West Cedar Street on Beacon Hill, Logue challenged the recently established Boston Redevelopment Authority to develop a vision for the city.

The BRA focused its attention on neighborhoods that could help revitalize the city's economy. One by one, these areas were transformed: Government Center in old Scollay Square (at the foot of Beacon Hill), a bolstered waterfront, a towering Prudential Center, a refurbished downtown business district, and a rehabilitated 502-acre Washington Park. These strides were warmly heralded. "Signs of Boston's hidden renaissance are beginning to multiply," reported the *Christian Science Monitor*, likening the situation to a butterfly emerging from its cocoon.[10]

But the new city was starting to look dramatically different from its predecessor. Unlike the redbrick low-rises of Beacon Hill and the former West End, concrete skyscrapers came to symbolize the new Boston, such as the Prudential Tower, rising fifty-two stories like a huge blue milk carton with a restaurant on top, and the cluster of twenty-two-story skyscrapers in the West End. Boston's provincial skyline was changing forever. Naturally, there were those who worried. Among them was Charles W. Eliot, a professor at Harvard's Graduate School of Design. "The towers of the 'new Boston' are almost all rectangular blocks chopped off at the maximum economic height," he lamented. For Eliot, the hallmark of Boston for over a century had been the gently rounded Beacon Hill, topped by Bulfinch's golden dome on the State House; the relatively uniform building height followed the shape of the ground. Many areas of Boston did need change, he conceded, but he strongly argued that Boston could "build on the success of the past without destroying our heritage."[11]

Like Eliot, residents of Beacon Hill watched the changes in Boston with mixed feelings. While the blight of the West End had been eliminated, so had some of the architectural consistency and harmony that had character-ized the neighborhood. For one thing, the gray skyscrapers of Charles River Park forcibly separated that neighborhood from Beacon Hill, making the Hill look like an island apart. The sense of isolation, Hillers now realized, might become more severe if the North Slope was itself to go the way of gray skyscrapers. The North Slope had long been a "poor sister," but it was now apparent to the Beacon Hillers that the poor sister had to be given attention. A real makeover was in store. The question was how to ensure that whatever was undertaken would not replace one form of blight with another, albeit more modern?

BATTLE FOR THE NORTH SLOPE

*T*HE Civic Association knew there was precedent for amending the 1955 bill that first created the Historic District of Beacon Hill. After three years, in 1958, it had amended the bill to include the Flat of the Hill. Now again, in February 1963, the Civic Association decided to sponsor legislation to make the North Slope a part of the historic neighborhood. This, the association hoped, would "preserve a vista of old Boston in the shadows of the new high-rise apartment buildings in the West End and the modern structures of the new Government Center." Though the North Slope had never been as grand or fashionable as the South, it nonetheless included some of the oldest and most important historic buildings on Beacon Hill. To the historically minded, at least, the North Slope's architecture blended beautifully with the Beacon Hill Historic District of the South Slope.[12]

To rally support for the new legislation, on February 25 a public meeting was held at St. John's Church on Bowdoin Street. The keynote speech came from Walter Muir Whitehill, a leading writer on Boston history and archi-tecture. Whitehill, the director of the Boston Athenaeum, was also chair of the Boston Historical Conservation Committee. The committee, he said, had determined that three buildings on the North Slope carried national significance: the Harrison Gray Otis house and the Old West Church, both on Cambridge Street, and the Egyptian revivalist building at 57 Hancock

Street. The proposal to include the North Slope, instantly embraced by Hillers, gave momentum to the forces of historical preservation.

In the State House, meanwhile, the legislation drew fierce opposition. At the center of the controversy was the future of Bowdoin Street, the eastern end of which had been demolished to make way for construction of the State Office Building.[13] The street had the longest row of bow-front Greek Revival housing from the 1840s and was considered a symbol of the transition between the modern buildings of Government Center and the redbrick colonials of Beacon Hill. To the residents of Beacon Hill, Bowdoin Street stood as a last line of defense against further encroachments from developers. Another view was held by commercial interests located on the street. All land on Bowdoin Street was under private ownership. One person alone owned nine parcels of land on the lower side of the street, and reportedly he was considering the construction of a new hotel or motel on the fringe of Government Center. Should the new legislation receive the approval of Massachusetts lawmakers, persons with such position and plans would be required to get permission from the Beacon Hill Architectural Commission before they could demolish bow-front buildings for any new construction.

Unfortunately for the forces of historical preservation, many House legislators were sympathetic to proposals for architecturally sensitive development of the desirable lower side of Bowdoin Street. The House voted down the bill, stating that it could be reconsidered only if the Bowdoin Street provision was omitted. The *Boston Sunday Globe*, calling the action "very discouraging," argued that omitting Bowdoin Street would destroy the line of transition between Government Center and Beacon Hill.

Despite immediate discouragement among Beacon Hill residents, the political currents running against North Slope preservation soon took a surprisingly reverse course. On May 22, 1963, the National Park Service of the Department of Interior gave the South Slope of Beacon Hill national visibility. The Park Service designated the South Slope a National Historic Landmark, one among sixty-five sites chosen in a new effort to commemorate American history. Representing Beacon Hill, Mayor Collins personally attended official ceremonies and received the award.[14] Somehow the honor seemed to presciently embrace the North Slope as well, like a powerful in-

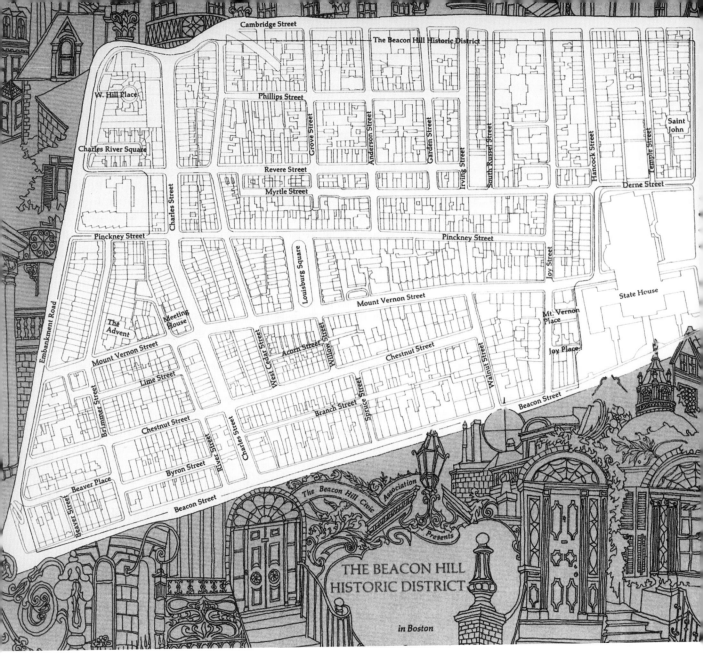

Beacon Hill Historic District. Courtesy of the Beacon Hill Civic Association.

visible hand reaching out to reclaim an endangered species. The effort to reconsider the bill for the preservation of the North Slope revived over the summer of 1963. It triumphed on August 9, when Governor Endicott Peabody signed a bill extending the Beacon Hill Historic District to include the North Slope. It had taken a five-month legislative battle. But there was no longer any question that Beacon Hill would be permanently preserved—not in part—but in its entirety.

TODAY'S INTERIOR, YESTERDAY'S WALL

T HE Beacon Hill Architectural Commission was, perhaps, destined to face hurricanes over modern development of the Hill. Things had started peacefully enough in the life of the young commission. In the eight years after its creation by the Massachusetts legislature in 1955, it had received more than two hundred applications from property owners seeking permission to renovate. The commission turned down very few of these proposals, since most would affect only interiors, and the mission of the Architectural Commission was to safeguard the exterior harmony of the Hill. Then came the spring of 1963. The architect Eduard Bullerjahn, a resident of Mount Vernon Street, and his partner, Andrew Hepburn, also an architect went looking for a certificate of demolition. They proposed tearing down the brownstone building at 70–72 Mount Vernon Street, built in 1846 by the esteemed architect Richard Upjohn.[15] The plan also called for demolishing

Granite chapel at 27–29 Chestnut Street, 1963. Courtesy of the *Boston Herald.* This chapel was formerly the Boston University School of Theology. A new proposal from the architects Bullerjahn and Hepburn called for the demolition of the chapel and the construction of luxury apartments. The proposal naturally resulted in a neighborhood uproar.

Andrew Hepburn (*left*) and his partner Eduard Bullerjahn, May 1963. Courtesy of the Associated Press. The two architects look over the plans of their proposed apartment complex.

the granite chapel at 27–29 Chestnut Street, formerly the home of the Boston University School of Theology. In the place of these buildings, Bullerjahn and Hepburn wanted to build a million-dollar complex of luxury apartments.

Apparently the architects were aware of the fact that proposals such as theirs could trigger passionate reactions among their fellow Beacon Hillers. Indeed, the prospect of obliterating buildings that had been around for as long as Louisburg Square caused the blood of many residents to boil. In this case Bullerjahn and Hepburn had secured the backing of some Boston heavyweights, which had the effect of splitting the Hill right down the middle. "Good heavens," lamented one resident, "old Boston friendships have broken over this."[16]

As the Beacon Hill Architectural Commission opened hearings, they listened as the parties made their cases. Supporting the plan was Walter Muir Whitehill, who had previously been known for his preservationist instincts. "Originally," Whitehill told the Architectural Commission, "these two brownstones represented the taste of newly-rich Boston merchants of the 19th century. They are grossly inharmonious with the small-brick structures of their neighbors."[17] Whitehill vouched for the character and competence of the two architects, stating his conviction that they would produce an apartment block that was architecturally sympathetic to neighboring buildings. Another supporter, eighty-six-year-old William Stanley Parker, an architect and former member of the Boston Planning Board, thought he could persuade the commission by suggesting that their initial reluctance had some historical irony: "These brownstones were built in 1846. If your commission were sitting at that time for the protection of the characteristics of Beacon Hill, [the brownstones] would never have been permitted to be built."[18] Another supporter of the new construction, Joseph Lund, a real estate executive and Hiller, said he could see no sound use for the present properties, except institutional, which was not in conformity with the area's residential character.

Opponents, like their adamant forebears in past battles over preservation, mounted an organized campaign, many of them canceling summer vacation plans. Ready to voice their views before the Architectural Commission,

Frederick Stahl, photograph by Christopher Morrow. The architect, a resident of Hancock Street, wrote a series of letters to the Beacon Hill Architectural Commission criticizing the Bullerjahn proposal as inconsistent with the adjacent buildings.

about 150 residents "marched down their historic citadel," reported the *Boston Globe*,[19] armed with nine hundred signatures opposing change. The opponents drew from the press comparisons to the "old Revolutionary rider with the red flag of warning" during the battles of Lexington and Concord.[20] Two spokesmen for the opposition, Carl Sapers and Jacob Atwood, reminded the commission of the statute prohibiting demolition and new construction. Bertram Little, director of the Society for the Preservation of New England Antiquities, also voiced the opposition of the society, recommending further exploration of new uses for the existing properties. Henry Milton, a professor of architectural history at MIT and a resident of Myrtle Street, declared, "This is no longer a local matter solely for the residents."[21] The Boston Society of Architects wrote to the Beacon Hill Architectural Commission and expressed their concern. Meanwhile the architect Frederick A. Stahl, a resident of Hancock Street, in a series of letters to the commission criticized the Bullerjahn proposal as inconsistent and inappropriate with the adjoining buildings. Also making her voice heard was Dorothy Upjohn Lewis, the great-granddaughter of the famed architect of the endangered Mount Vernon brownstone. Writing the commission from her home in Long Island, she stated her hope that "valiant Bostonians" would save their Beacon Hill buildings from "the Hunnish hordes of progress."[22]

The Beacon Hill Architectural Commission was left with the unenviable task of deciding what to do. On August 21, 1963, the commission pleased the opposition forces by rejecting the Bullerjahn-Hepburn proposal. However, the commission still left the door ajar for alternative plans. And alternative plans did emerge from the same architects. This time Bullerjahn and Hepburn proposed thirty-one modern luxury apartments within the shells of old structures, suggesting that the finished buildings could be "1840s on the outside" and "1960s on the inside." Bullerjahn argued that with modern technology the buildings would be so soundproof that "a child sleeping in one room would not be disturbed by someone in an adjoining room playing a grand piano."[23] The apartments would also have individually controlled air-conditioning, enabling residents to enjoy today's interior within yesterday's walls. Hillers welcomed the new prospect. This time, breathing a sigh of relief, the Beacon Hill Architectural Commission gave the green light.

TOWN AND GOWN

*L*IKE a first wave of settlers that brings another wave, Bullerjahn and Hepburn were but the first of many new incursions into Beacon Hill in 1963. For some time Suffolk University had been eyeing the eastern border of the North Slope. Suffolk, the largest institutional neighbor of Beacon Hill, that year purchased land on Temple Street, the former home of the First Methodist Church, as well as the Temple Hall Hotel and a small apartment house. A few years later, the university also bought 32 and 34 Hancock Street, two buildings destroyed by fire the previous winter. The plan was to demolish existing buildings and turn the property into a student parking lot. In the meantime the university also took an interest in the abandoned Stop & Shop building on Cambridge Street. These aggressive moves by what used to be a quiet neighbor created fears that the residential character of the Hill was again being threatened. This fear intensified when Hillers learned that the legislature was considering an amendment to the bill that originally protected the North Slope as a Historic District, an amendment that would exempt Suffolk from architectural controls on the district—granting it a variance. The traditionally peaceful relationship of "town and gown," as the *Beacon Hill News* termed it, was now in jeopardy.[24]

Perhaps the main difficulty for the Hill was the perception of the North

123

Slope held by university students and officials. "Suffolk is located on the 'dark side' of the Hill," wrote the student government president to the *Boston Globe*. "We are not discussing the beautiful 19th century homes on Mt. Vernon Street or Louisburg Square. We are discussing the buildings located on lower Joy Street, Hancock Street, and Temple Street. These are a series of antiquated, run-down apartment houses which in no way can be called worthy examples of early architecture."[25] An editorial in the school newspaper, the *Suffolk Journal*, echoed that sentiment. "There is nothing historic or charming about this area. It looks older than God, and life there is as stark and as harsh as in Hell."[26] Residents of the North Slope, of course, took exception to such views, considering their neighborhood nothing less than a precious memorial to the past, as well as a place to which young couples were bringing renewal.[27]

In December 1967 rising tempers turned into a pitched battle. The Boston Board of Appeals gave Suffolk University a variance to go ahead and convert the one-story building, the former Stop & Shop, into a five-story, multipurpose undergraduate facility. In response, the Beacon Hill Civic Association formed a special planning committee chaired by Frederick Stahl of Hancock Street and James McNeely of Temple Street. The committee tried to work out a compromise with all parties involved.[28] When negotiations failed, both town and gown threw down their gauntlets and went to court. Representing the Civic Association was the association's former president, Gael Mahony of the law firm Hill and Barlow. The case of *Trustees of Suffolk University* v. *James McNeely et al.* proved a long and costly legal battle. To raise funds for indefinite court proceedings, the association reached out to its members.[29] They delivered. By the summer of 1970 there was good news. On July 3 the Supreme Judicial Court of the Commonwealth decided in favor of the association's appeal, denying the granting of a variance to Suffolk University. Once again the integrity of Beacon Hill and its future as a residential community had been reaffirmed.

THE SUMMER OF LOVE

THE 1960s that swept Beacon Hill into battles to preserve local turf also swept Hillers into controversy over much larger conflicts. By the summer of 1967 more than half a million American soldiers had gone to fight in Vietnam, thirteen thousand of them killed in action. American public sentiment toward the war began to turn from initial ambivalence to open protest. On October 16 Boston joined forty other American cities as a venue for simultaneous antiwar rallies. More than five thousand participants, mostly students and faculty from Greater Boston and other New England colleges, gathered on Boston Common. Speakers at the rally included Professor Noam Chomsky of the Massachusetts Institute of Technology and Professor Howard Zinn of Boston University. More than one hundred ministers from various denominations also joined in. "We are now in effect declaring our independence from this war," said Professor Zinn to a youthful, orderly audience sitting shoulder-to-shoulder on the Common.[30] "The men who went to war most often and died most frequently were the people who had nothing to gain."

After the rally demonstrators, led by a coalition of ministers, marched to Arlington Street Church. The church soon overflowed, and three thousand people were left standing outside. Inside, speakers elaborated the religious and moral justifications of civil disobedience. Invoking Socrates and Saint Peter, the Reverend William Sloan Coffin, Jr., chaplain of Yale University and cochairman of the National Committee of Clergy and Laymen Concerned about Vietnam, suggested that each student must probe his own conscience to justify civil disobedience. "Men at times will feel constrained to disobey the law out of a sense of obedience to a higher allegiance," said the Reverend Coffin. At the conclusion of speeches, Dr. George H. Williams of Harvard Divinity School signaled students to burn their draft cards. Fifty-six young men marched to the altar as a hushed crowd looked on. A burning candle on the altar was used to ignite their draft cards. Another 214 students decided to give their cards to the clergy of their respective faiths to be taken to Washington and turned over to U.S. Attorney General Ramsey Clark. The students were ready to accept whatever action the federal government would take. Jail was not to be feared, said Ray Mungo, the former editor of the *Boston University News* and a graduate student at Harvard. Jail was an honorable alternative to serving in Vietnam. Church bells pealed out the tune to "We Shall Overcome."

More than two hundred faculty members from New England colleges also pledged their allegiance to draft resisters and signed a declaration of support in a newspaper advertisement. "As their teachers," said the declaration, "we stand with them to help in any way we can. . . . We can and do pledge them our total support."[31] Many residents of Beacon Hill also registered their support. Led by Joseph Masski, a real estate agent living on Revere Street, a group of young Hillers formed the Beacon Hill Committee on the

Antiwar demonstration by clergymen in front of the State House, May 5, 1970, photograph by Ulrike Welsch of the *Herald Traveler*. Courtesy of the Boston Public Library.

War in Vietnam. Their goal was to educate the public about the war and its adverse impact on American life. The committee also planned to persuade local political leaders to work for an end to the war.[32] Canvassing the Hill door-to-door with a public opinion poll, they found that 60 to 70 percent of Hillers opposed the war. Antiwar efforts of the Beacon Hillers were augmented by the formation of another group of protesters, known as the Beacon Hill Support Group for Peace Action in Vietnam, which used the Charles Street Meeting House as its headquarters. They distributed antiwar literature and organized citizen participation in many peace rallies, including the 1969 national antiwar rally in Washington, D.C.[33]

Beacon Hill was deeply affected by the emerging "youth culture" during the antiwar movement, as it attracted, like a magnet, many rebellious youth who defied tradition. As elsewhere, these young people were driven by a mix of motivations—on the one hand, ideals of equality, nonexploitation, and reverence for the sacredness of life; on the other hand, a deeply troubled sense over events in Southeast Asia. Some wanted to develop a more defined "counterculture," taking cues from university intellectuals. And like their cohorts in other parts of the country, many of those involved on the Hill were youth caught up in the throes of late adolescence, interpreting the call to counterculture as an occasion to free themselves from any social or parental constraint and to experiment with free love and drugs. These were the "hippies" of Beacon Hill.

Charles Street, the main commercial thoroughfare, became the center of "youthful" activities on the Hill. Groups of young people loitered day and night at store entrances and street corners, some wearing "Dutch-boy hats on unwashed hair."[34] The blockage of traffic disturbed the residents and shopkeepers, as did the dirtied streets. In time, customers were discouraged from shopping on Charles Street, and some stores were forced to close. In fact, Charles Street was in real trouble, wrote the *Beacon Hill News*. "Shopping center, playground, combat zone, public dump, or historic showplace: what is the future of Charles Street?"[35] Drug trafficking was on the rise, not only on the main street but also throughout Beacon Hill. The police station on Joy Street became an unwilling, temporary stop for those unable to get away when the police showed up. Describing the situation with an overtone of humor, an article appeared in the *Beacon Hill News:* "The pot-head was inside the temporary lock-up room, his hands trussed behind him with his own vest. Bearded, shoeless and semi-toothless. Earlier that evening he had tried serenading Beacon Hill. Unfortunately, no one appreciated his efforts, especially since the concert had blocked traffic on Phillips Street."[36]

The use of marijuana, LSD, and other drugs on Beacon Hill increased so fast that Beacon Hill unwillingly gained a reputation as one of Boston's leading drug traffic centers. During the summer of 1967, the "hippie summer," thousands of migrating youth brought a kind of Haight-Ashbury atmosphere to the Boston Common and Beacon Hill, as drug dealers set up shop for major trafficking. Window boxes on the Hill were used as stashes for cocaine. Burglary and related crimes followed. Many residents, according to the *Beacon Hill News*, hoped that "a strong breeze or a Harvard riot" might "dislodge the gypsies."[37]

Beacon Hill's response to the new hippie culture was as diverse as the hippie culture itself. There were hard-liners calling for police control of hippies and a curfew on the Common. There were soft-liners who sympathized with the younger generation and tried to reach out to them with medical, psychiatric, and other social services. There were also middle-of-the-roaders, advocating medical assistance to the needy coupled with increased law enforcement and street clearance. Many Hill residents tried to distinguish the idealist hippies from the junkies. "We 'squares' have no mission to be critical of the clothes and habits of the hippie population, nor of their philosophy," wrote Frederick Witherby, president of the Beacon Hill Civic Association, "because the principles of American life are based upon the right of each individual to make a personal choice as to certain matters so long as he does not interfere with the rights of other people."[38] Long hair and idleness were their business, said Maurice E. Frye, Jr., a state representative, "but pan-handling, litter-bugging, using and trafficking drugs, blocking public ways, and over-use of public parks are my business."[39]

In fact, many Hill residents made it their own business to try to deal with the unruly situation. As early as 1963, three like-minded neighbors, Nathaniel Young and Nicholas DeWolf of Pinckney Street and John Ryan of West Cedar Street, had formed a three-man Law Enforcement Committee to supervise the streets and curb disturbances with the police department. The three-member committee gained financial support from fourteen other residents on the North Slope. After making house-to-house calls, the committee appointed six street captains with the principal duties of disseminating the committee's literature and organizing residents of their streets. A hotline and a designated mailbox were established to encourage residents to report disturbances. During the summer of 1967, a four-man police foot patrol was added, covering the Charles Street area after 6 P.M., and charged with, in addition to normal parking and traffic enforcement, breaking up gangs of hippies gathered in store entrances or across sidewalks. By the summer of 1969, a small group of North Slope residents formed what they called the "North Slope Average Neighbors Group," trying to remedy conditions that threatened health and safety on the North Slope. The same summer, the Hip Task Force was also established to provide free programs of recreation and entertainment to the large influx of youth.[40]

But if there were efforts to curb disruptions of peace and order, there also surfaced a recognition that serious needs existed among the hippie community—needs that Hillers could and should do something about. The Old West Church held weekly dialogue forums for community leaders, including the mayor's office, the police department, medical and social workers, and other concerned citizens. Out of these meetings came the formation of a Youth Hostel, all-night drop-in centers in two local churches, and professional counseling for many hippies. Such solutions, many believed, would have a better long-term impact than jails, mental institutions, and remedial programs. The Reverend Hudson, copastor of Old West Church, observed later that some recognized that the failures of what was called the "silent generation" had actually helped create the conditions that produced these young people.[41]

Another effort to generate creative solutions came from Dr. Alfred Koumans, a psychiatrist at both Massachusetts Institute of Technology and Massachusetts General Hospital, and Dr. David Lewis, an internist at Beth Israel Hospital. They both took an interest in addressing the deteriorating health of hippies, many of whom tended to refuse medical help even when suffering from ulcerative colitis, pneumonia, kidney infections, and acute psychosis. Some of the needier hippies found their way to volunteer organizations such as Project Place, a halfway house for troubled youth run by divinity students in the South End. But basic medical assistance was lacking at Project Place. Following the model of a free clinic in San Francisco, Dr. Koumans and Dr. Lewis set out to establish their own free clinic, called Medical Service, in the summer of 1968. Koumans and Lewis believed that the best location for the clinic, if it was to be accessible and effective, would be close to Boston Common, where most hippies congregated. The doctors settled, ironically, upon a site widely perceived to be one of the city's most conservative establishments—King's Chapel, courtesy of the Reverend Carl Scovel, its pastor. Scovel persuaded members of his Board of Regents to allow the doctors to use the Parish House at 64 Beacon Street for the summer.[42]

As word got out about the new free clinic, volunteers began to pour in from local hospitals, including internists, pediatricians, psychiatrists, social workers, nurses, and medical students. The clinic soon had a staff of sixty people, with more on the waiting list. All except for a full-time secretary served without pay. Hospitals, medical supply companies, and drug companies rushed free supplies to the clinic. The Massachusetts Mental Health Association furnished whatever supplies were needed that had not been donated. Financial donations came in from Hill residents and members of King's Chapel. During the summer of 1968, the free clinic was able to treat 450 patients, most between fourteen and twenty-four years old and suffering problems ranging from minor infections to serious disease. A friendly rapport was taking hold among hippie patients and the medical staff, especially as the clinic demonstrated it could strictly observe confidentiality. Meanwhile, the Reverend Scovel and church volunteers made food coupons available to those in need. "You don't have to be a hippie to treat hippies," concluded Dr. Lewis. "It is only when older people make up their minds beforehand and start acting like parents that the kids run away. We treat them without moral judgments."[43]

Success notwithstanding, the clinic was controversial among Hillers. Supporters said it fulfilled humanitarian imperatives—for hippies had their rights too. Others worried the clinic would attract even more hippies to the area. At one meeting of the Civic Association, a resident called the effort to provide aid and comfort to drug users a "cruel betrayal" of those who lived on

Hill House (old firehouse), 127 Mount Vernon Street, 2001. In order to expand and serve the community better, Hill House purchased the old firehouse. Countless volunteers worked tirelessly to make the new Hill House a true community center for all the residents of Beacon Hill.

Church of the Advent, Mount Vernon and Brimmer Streets, 2002, photograph by the author.

The "Sunflower House," 2002, photograph by the author. The house at 130 Mount Vernon Street was built in 1840 and remodeled in 1878.

ABOVE AND RIGHT: Louisburg Square at dawn, 2002, photograph by the author.

Acorn Street, 2002, photograph by the author. In the nineteenth century the cobblestone street became home to many servants working for the families of the South Slope. This may be the most often photographed street on Beacon Hill.

Christmas decorations, 2001, photograph by the author. West Cedar Street is dressed up for the season.

Students standing outside the Advent School, the only independent elementary school on Beacon Hill. Courtesy of Nancy Harris Frohlich.

Beacon Hill. In his view, drug traffic had turned the neighborhood into a slum, so that it was not safe any more to send children to the Common or to leave wives at home alone. The Reverend William Alberts of Old West Church countered by characterizing that position as one marked by hysteria and dehumanization. "These young people are still human beings," he said.[44] Among the 150 members on hand, there were cheers for arguments on both sides of the issue.

The hippie era served as a mirror for the community to reflect on its own attitudes, value systems, and humanity, a process that went on for several summers to come. In his letter to the *Beacon Hill News*, the Reverend Hudson tried to put the hippie experience into perspective. The widespread breakdown of American home life, he said, along with the search to replace old systems of authority with authenticity and integrity, and the unrest among young people concerning war, poverty, and injustice, their idealism and the possibility of a more human society—all these suggested that the "youth problem" would be around for many years to come. "Perhaps we would be well advised in some areas to wish them well." One possible solution to the hippie problem, argued Hudson, was to try to be more sensitive to the individuals who got lumped into this group. "They really do not make up a single type any more than the 'straight' citizens of Beacon Hill make up a single type."[45]

If one thing was certain about Beacon Hill residents, they simply all did not hold the same image of "hippies." It was equally true that they did not agree on what to do about them. The hippie summer passed, like other summers, never to return in its original form. But many of the realizations born during that summer—both sympathetic and defensive—continued to reverberate for many years.

THE '60s GENERATION DIGS IN

IN THE 1960s three momentous social developments converged on American life—the antiwar movement, the Civil Rights movement, and the youth counterculture. Each in its own way brought to the surface contradictions in American life that had long been repressed or denied. How to reconcile the fact that in this democracy persons of diverse races and colors were not being treated equally? How, in the wealthiest nation on earth, could so many citizens be living in poverty? How could a nation that espoused the moral and spiritual values of great religious traditions experience such disintegration of family and community? By the 1970s the young people who had openly and rebelliously brought these contradictions to light now faced the challenge of rebuilding a society based on truer ideals.

Beacon Hill, in its own search for answers, was slowly being transformed. Since the 1960s the Hill had witnessed a major demographic change, with a growing number of young people in their twenties and early thirties moving to the Hill. By 1970 that number had risen 40 percent compared to 1960.[46] Some in this age group had experienced the Vietnam War firsthand. Those who had not been to Vietnam were still deeply influenced by the ethos of the period. Most of them brought to Beacon Hill a heightened sense of volunteerism, as well as the desire to find a broader, more inclusive sense of community—even if it meant challenging some practices of the revered Civic Association.

Nick DeWolf, for one, felt that the long-standing gap between the association and the community had widened into a gulf. In the fall of 1970 he called for a dramatic shift in the association's orientation and attitude. Joining DeWolf in his concerns was Bernard Borman, a resident of 3 Rollins Place, a former president of the association, and a lawyer with the firm Nathanson and Rudofsky. They urged the association to do more—in light of the mounting urban crisis across America—to encourage democratic participation in the association. Looking at the nominated candidates for leadership of the association for 1970, Borman pointed out that no one had been nominated from seven major streets of the North Slope. Questions needed to be asked, said Borman. How many tenants were being nominated? How many under thirty? Or twenty? How many poor folks? How many nonwhites? "It is no excuse," he said, "to say that these people don't participate in the Beacon Hill Civic Association. Their nonparticipation in community affairs is the root of the problem on Beacon Hill." Term limits should also be imposed, in Borman's view, to avoid the appearance of "musical chairs" and self-perpetuating "clubism." In short, Borman argued, in an era in which neighborhoods all over America were demonstrating new abilities to organize and be heard, Beacon Hill, with its heterogeneous composition and well-educated citizenry, should have one of the most progressive and broadly based neighborhood associations. Membership recruitment should be drawn from all geographic areas, among all ethnic groups, age groups, owners, and tenants.[47]

While Bernard Borman and Nick DeWolf were shaking things up in the Civic Association, an attempt to build a more inclusive neighborhood was taking place on other fronts as well, some with roots going back to the 1960s. In 1966 there came up for sale the old police office, known as Station Three, at 74 Joy Street. Built in 1862 by the City of Boston, the building had had a colorful history. During World War II stopping at Station Three became a "must" activity for servicemen, since both the Navy Shore Patrol and the Army Military Police were headquartered there. Failing to stop in would be like coming to see Boston and failing to pay one's respects to the Bunker Hill Monument or Paul Revere's house. Station Three continued its fame after the war. John F. Kennedy once voted there. Willie Sutton, a famous robber, slept there, as did a murderer brought back all the way from Carson City, Nevada, by a Mounties-like police chief. No criminal had ever succeeded in breaking out of Station Three.

For the Beacon Hill Civic Association the sale of Station Three loomed as a major opportunity for community service and inclusion. The association decided to bid on the property, intending to convert it to a community center and a permanent home for the association and the Beacon Hill Nursery School. Plans also included a recreation center with a comprehensive program for senior citizens on the Hill, gym facilities for classes from the Advent School, and after-school activities for all youngsters of the Hill. This was one Hill initiative that seemed to attract universal support from the neighbors, as well as the city at large. Police Commissioner Edmund McNamara and Mayor John Collins endorsed the sale of the building to the association. State Senator Oliver Ames and State Representatives John W. Sears, Maurice Frye, Jr., and Katherine Kane spoke in favor at a hearing before the Boston City Council. All emphasized the idea that the center would be available to *all* residents of the neighborhood.[48] In March 1966 the city council gave its final approval.[49] And in May of the same year, the new community center was officially incorporated as Hill House, with a twenty-one-member board of directors.

HILL HOUSE

JOSEPH LUND was sure Beacon Hill had reached a real turning point, a moment at which a community makes a decision that forever changes its direction. Lund and Guido Perera were cochairs of the 1966 Capital Fund Drive for Hill House. "Our neighborhood," said Lund, "which decided a decade ago to embrace the Historic District (a decision whose beneficial effects are still being felt), now has another opportunity of comparable magnitude. It is a chance to develop here on Beacon Hill a unique community center financed by, run by and for the benefit of all of the people of Beacon Hill."[50] Hill House, like the Historic District legislation, became a vehicle for realizing a shared vision, one that reflected the spirit of the times. In its Articles of Organization, Hill House was described as serving the needs of all residents of Beacon Hill, old and young. This all-inclusiveness became its hallmark. Its objectives were "to progress towards elimination of poverty or causes of poverty among persons in the Beacon Hill neighborhood" and "to alleviate the problems of aging by providing new learning and service opportunities for the senior citizens of Beacon Hill."[51] The idealism of the 1960s and the generation that shaped and was shaped by it became the driving force behind this new communal vision.

With song and dance Hill House officially opened on October 22, 1968, after two years of renovation. The nursery school moved into its new quarters with a play yard that charmed parents[52] and a full enrollment of more than seventy children between the ages of two and five. With the new facility, the school was poised for a program expansion, adding afternoon classes to its original mornings-only curriculum. Beacon Hill's "native-grown" teenagers were also beneficiaries of Hill House. Inspired by the success of a teen program of Old West Church, the board of Hill House voted to appropriate funds for the church to start a similar program at Hill House.

Serving only the teenagers of Beacon Hill and Charles River Park, the new Beacon Hill Teen Program offered a variety of activities, including athletics and courses on television production with video expert Steve Gilford. An open shop program with Tom Wilson of Asterisk, where teens over fifteen could design their own projects (ham radio, woodwork, auto mechanics), as well as dance lessons for four days a week with live bands and refreshments, were offered.

Adult volunteers, in addition to being chaperones, were encouraged to reach out to the teenagers as friends and advise them on both personal and school-related issues.[53] At a time when many teenagers were turning to drugs as a form of rebellion, Hill House created a sanctuary in an effort to channel the boundless energies of teenagers into more positive activities.

Other programs benefited adults, including more than a thousand senior citizens, a group for whom few services had been offered on the Hill. A large area at the front of Hill House was designated the reading and recreation

Karate training at Hill House, 1970s. Courtesy of Hill House.

lounge for senior citizens. It was furnished with games and reading materials, along with information on Medicare, Social Security, health lectures, and trips to historic spots. The senior citizens, feeling more connected with each other and their community, soon began to make joint decisions, such as voting to join the National Council of Senior Citizens.

Meanwhile, young adults also made good use of course offerings at Hill House, which included lectures on Beacon Hill architecture, Italian language, history, and the arts.

The role of Hill House went beyond providing a shared physical space; it offered a vehicle to reach out to a broader spectrum of neighbors who called Beacon Hill home.

CHARLES STREET FAIR

ONE crisp fall day in 1970, a happier wind blew across Beacon Hill, as if to say that the heaviness of the times would not be allowed to utterly flatten Boston spirits: neighbors celebrated the first Charles Street Fair. It was the genesis of a new-fashioned tradition, one that would last well into the next decade.[54] Community institutions had joined together in the planning—the Beacon Hill Garden Club, Hill House, the Beacon Hill Nursery School, among others. Young and old were entertained by a mix of offerings, from carnival games, to book and bake sales, to the demonstration of a full-sized sailboat by the Charles River Boating Club. Colorful banners adorned the Charles Street Hardware Store to attract public attention.[55] To recruit members for the association, a large map of Beacon Hill was displayed with red dots showing where current members lived. By the end of the fair, seventy-five more red dots had been added.[56] Ideas were hatched that would enhance the fair in years to come: the ideas of creating a beer garden, a flea market, a raffle with prizes, and arts and entertainment. What began as a rather modest effort became, by 1976, an event attracting thirty thousand visitors, with local television stations covering the activities for the nightly news.

For Hillers the Charles Street Fair was a reminder that a little community

Charles Street Fair, 1970s. Courtesy of the Beacon Hill Civic Association. Started in the fall of 1970, the Charles Street Fair became a celebrated neighborhood affair and a Beacon Hill tradition until 1988, when it was canceled.

spirit could do wonders not just for renewing the neighborhood, but also for keeping businesses in the area. From the early days local merchants showed their enthusiasm for the idea by offering donations, free services, and supplies. The participants' list came to read like a business directory of Beacon Hill, with names such as the Massachusetts Eye and Ear Infirmary, Stop & Shop, Phillips Drug Store, Kelley's Ice Cream, Nino's Pizza, and Baskin-Robbins. The fair was, in one sense, an expression of the Hillers' desire to reclaim their main street from the aftermath of the Vietnam War. And businesses also renewed their faith in the Hill, especially its main street.

A "sister fair," meanwhile, made its debut in the spring of 1975. At "Health-Fest," sponsored by the Massachusetts Eye and Ear Infirmary and the Beacon Hill Civic Association, Hill residents of all ages were invited to receive free medical exams and advice. Doctors, nurses, and hospital staff from the Infirmary were on hand to advise and screen for eye, ear, nose, and throat problems, while other local health groups held workshops on resuscitating victims of heart attacks. At the corner of Fruit and Charles Streets strolling performers and musicians entertained patients and visitors. More than eight hundred people sampled the free screening that day, with Beacon Hill's elderly being special beneficiaries. Massachusetts General Hospital joined the sponsorship the following year, offering free screenings for blood pressure, as well as measuring height and weight. Educational booths and a film series provided other essential health information. Between HealthFest and the Charles Street Fair, the effects in the postwar period were apparently therapeutic; boundaries had begun to fall between rich and poor, old and young, in the celebration of common humanity and neighborliness.

In 1978 more than forty thousand people visited the Charles Street Fair, making it the largest neighborhood street fair in Boston.[57] Organizers sensed they had something extraordinary on their hands. Like Christmas Eve on the Hill a few decades before, the Charles Street Fair was becoming a Beacon Hill tradition in its own right, even a *Boston* tradition. "The Charles Street Fair isn't ours alone anymore," commented the *Beacon Hill News*.[58] Publicity brought larger and larger crowds from out of town, making it nearly impossible to walk across the streets on fair day. The sheer size started to make the event more and more unwieldy as years went on. By the mid-

Charles Street Fair, 1980s. Courtesy of the Beacon Hill Civic Association. The Charles Street Fair became the largest of its kind in Boston, visited by more than forty thousand people.

1980s, insurance costs had quadrupled. In 1986 the beer garden was canceled because no insurance company was willing to provide host-liquor liability insurance. In an effort to avoid the throngs, more and more of Beacon Hill's own residents stayed away. The goal of "neighboring," which first brought the fair into existence, seemed to have been lost sight of, as larger forces of urban reveling set in. In 1988 the Civic Association finally decided to cancel the Charles Street Fair and refocus on the Winter Ball, which was started in 1972 to celebrate the fiftieth anniversary of the Civil Association, as the major annual event for the Hill and its community.

SMALL MIRACLES

SINCE the Mount Vernon Proprietors put their first ad in the *Columbian Centinel* in 1796 to attract new residents, only two types of accommodations existed on Beacon Hill: owner-occupied, single-family houses and rooming houses. Traditionally, each rooming house was presided over and cared for by a widow, known as a "mother hen"—this was a way for widows to supplement their income. Lodgers tended to stay a long time and were considered either part of her family or permanent guests. Through the caring hands of mother hens on the Hill, rooming houses were generally kept clean and orderly. By the early 1970s, however, though some of the traditional rooming houses still existed, more and more had come to be managed by commercial syndicated trusts and absentee owners who invested little in property maintenance. Increasingly, tenants of the rooming houses were transients.

In the mid-1970s a new urban housing fad found its way to Beacon Hill in the form of converting apartments and single-family houses into condominiums. Baby boomers and young urban professionals (yuppies) were attracted to the idea because condos satisfied both their urge to own property at a relatively low cost and their preference for city living. Two entire buildings on Hancock Street, for example, were converted into condo units. The full-floor, two-bedroom units, twelve in all, were sold before they were finished at forty to fifty thousand dollars per unit. With both excitement and concern, the residents watched this new real estate phenomenon spread across Beacon Hill.

In February 1976 the *Beacon Hill News* investigated the community's view toward it. "Is this the beginning of a trend that can save once lavish single-family houses from absentee landlords?" asked the newspaper. "Is it a means by which middle-class families can afford to own properties on Beacon Hill?" At first, many Hillers saw the condo conversions as a solution to some long-standing problems on the Hill. Ownership of property, they believed, would lead to pride and upkeep for buildings and the neighborhood, motivated by the financial commitments involved. The streets of Beacon Hill would be cleaner and safer. But as condo conversion spread, attitudes began to change. From 1976 to 1978 the number of condo conversions went up a whopping 200 percent, starting to leave what, for some, was a worrisome imprint on the Hill.[59] Some were concerned that the conversions were leaving fewer apartments on the Hill, driving up their rents, forcing some elderly and less affluent families to move out, and further gentrifying the neighborhood. Other neighbors worried that condo conversion could threaten the existence of single-family houses. Still others were troubled to see some long-term residents forced out of Beacon Hill because they were either unable or unwilling to buy.

In a humorous though impassioned article, twenty-eight-year-old resident Chris Glynn wrote about his own experience in the five years since 1973. In those years Glynn lived in an apartment with his housemate, Susan. "We intended to continue to live together, until death or marriage do us part," Glynn wrote. "We thought about death and marriage. We didn't think about condominium conversion." The couple's residence had now been sold and rumor had it that all in the building would be forcibly "converted" to condominiums. "I do not wish to convert," protested Glynn. However, if necessary, he said, he would try to buy, which would mean "going into hock *majeur* when neither of us wants to or really is ready to." Condo conversion, admitted Glynn, most certainly had its good points. But the negatives heavily outweighed the benefits. The Hill, he said, would become an upper-class ghetto, with all the implied sterility. "Anything worth converting was on the danger list, leaving only the small, dark, dank, and bug-ridden apartments for the masses. The landed gentry will move into the bigger boxes, and the rest of us will get the pigeon coops."[60]

Chris Glynn was not alone in his feelings about condos. Shirley Thatcher had worked for many years with programs to assist the elderly on the Hill. It was getting more and more difficult, she said, to find rooms on the first and second floors for senior citizens with physical disabilities. According to a list compiled by the Civic Association in 1976, forty licensed lodging houses existed on the Hill, with 70 percent of the tenants being elderly or nonprofessionals who had lived there for a long time.[61] Beacon Hill had always comprised a diverse mix of Brahmins, professionals, itinerants, and the poor. "The viability of any community is its ability to integrate its different segments," argued Thatcher.[62]

Sharing the concerns of Thatcher and Glynn was the new president of the Civic Association, Joel Pierce. As the oldest neighborhood organization in America, he wrote, the association was strongly interested in preserving the special character of life on the Hill as an economically mixed residential neighborhood. "I personally prefer a policy that would severely restrict conversion where elderly, low-income, or handicapped tenants would be displaced." But it was an intriguing question, reported the *Beacon Hill News:* how could something that is "so good for the neighborhood . . . be bad for the neighborhood at the same time?"[63] The task of reconciling the desire for neighborhood diversity, on the one hand, with the rights of property owners, on the other, was now turned over to a special housing policy subcommittee of the Civic Association. In time, other members of the Civic Association also volunteered their time and expertise, creating several proud "miracles" on the Hill.

The old Bowdoin School was the first of the Hill's new stories of realized hope. Constructed in 1896 on Myrtle Street, the building served as an elementary school for Beacon Hill and the West End until 1936, when the Boston School Committee moved in its administrative offices. Later, as the new City Hall was under construction in the mid-1960s, it became apparent that the School Committee would relocate into the new City Hall, triggering renewed speculation about the future of the old school building. Would there now be luxury apartments? Or what? The Civic Association immediately voted down the idea of luxury units in favor of serving the housing needs of senior citizens on the North Slope. The City of Boston, for its part, furnished public funds to encourage the conversion of properties into subsidized housing for the elderly and poor.

Most important, though, were the volunteer initiatives of people like Bernard Borman, a former president of the Civic Association, and Roy Littlehale, a realtor and chairman of the association's Bowdoin School Committee. Together with other volunteers from the Hill, Borman and Littlehale brought their expertise in real estate and politics to bear and negotiated with the city to acquire the old school building at a reasonable price. They also worked out terms with private developers for renovation and collaborated with the public and private sectors to find creative financing options.[64] The architect Frederick Stahl was brought in to conduct a feasibility study on the architectural viability of converting the building into apartments. And once Borman and Littlehale got the green light from the architect, they found a developer and launched construction.[65]

As the renovation went forward, the former school was transformed into thirty-five apartments on five floors, twenty of them one-bedroom units, the rest two-bedroom units, and space was set aside for a community meeting room and lounge. Plans were drawn up for rents to be reasonable and for some apartments to qualify for rent subsidies.[66] August 25, 1977, saw the official opening of the Bowdoin School Apartments. On this cool, sunny, late-summer day, a large crowd gathered at the newly renovated apartments for the ceremony, including Hill residents, city officials, architects, planners, and new tenants. One of those present that day, Stephen Oleskey, later reflected that the new project demonstrated what a volunteer association could do to enhance an urban neighborhood.[67] Bowdoin School Apartments was also an important watershed for the generation that came of age in the 1960s. As John Bok, a resident of Pinckney Street, later reminisced, the project embodied the ideal of the 1960s generation to realize a more inclusive and diverse vision of community.[68] The *Beacon Hill News* called the completed work "a small miracle."[69]

Another neighborhood miracle occurred just a few years later. Two blocks away from the State House, at the corner of Myrtle and Joy Streets, stood

The Beacon Chambers Hotel, in an 1898 rendering. Courtesy of the *Boston Herald*. Designed by the architect Herbert Hale, the hotel was built as a rooming house at Joy and Myrtle Streets.

the five-story Beacon Chambers, an apartment complex for 350 elderly men of low income. In 1980 a midday fire ravaged the building. The men's lives were spared, but all were left homeless. The site was considered a prime location for high-end condominiums. Beacon Chambers became the focus of developers interested in converting the damaged structure, as had been the Bowdoin School building.

As it had with the Bowdoin School, the community intervened. A group of former residents of Beacon Chambers filed a class-action suit in the Boston Housing Court, requesting the right to reclaim the units. A Housing Court judge, George Daher, ruled in their favor. The majority of the Beacon Hill residents expressed their desire for the building to remain a

The Beacon Chambers
Hotel on fire, October 14,
1980. Courtesy of the
Boston Herald. A midday
fire ravaged the hotel, leaving 350 elderly men of low
income unharmed but
homeless. Shown here are
firefighters rescuing residents from the building.

sanctuary for elderly and low-income residents. The Rogerson House of Jamaica Plain, a well-endowed, elder-care organization with 130 years of history, indicated its willingness to purchase the building and restore it to moderate-income housing. With the support of the Civic Association, the Rogerson House acquired financing from the Massachusetts Housing Finance Agency and other government sources. Beacon Hill residents also contributed money and time to make the project possible.

Three years after the fire that demolished the old site, the new Beacon House opened its doors. Its atrium, topped by a skylight and its eight stories of tiered brick balconies, graced the entrance of the House. As its executive director, James F. Seagle, Jr., would later explain, the realization of this 6.6-million-dollar project showed that low-income people could indeed live side by side with the well-to-do if a community made that decision. The *Boston Globe*, in a story entitled "A Beacon of Hope," exclaimed that housing for single people of modest means had been preserved and enhanced, even on some of the choicest real estate in the heart of Boston. Not every project had well-to-do neighbors of conscience who would contribute to it, added the *Globe*, noting that in many places such neighbors typically opposed subsidized housing. The reopening of the old Beacon Chambers signaled that Beacon Hill wanted to remain a true urban center, a place where people of diverse economic status could reside in dignity.[70]

BEACON HILL VILLAGE IN THE NEW MILLENNIUM

THE turn of the twenty-first century again found the citizens of Beacon Hill shaping new forms of community life. Just as one group had launched a diversified retirement community in the 1980s through subsidized housing, another group would now envision a second alternative in retirement living. Appropriately named Beacon Hill Village, the new concept involved creating a private, nonprofit organization to help its members enjoy their later years to the fullest in their own homes by providing them with the practical means and assistance. The concept entailed a modest annual membership fee. Participants would then be entitled to a package of services ranging from social and cultural activities to multiple options for exercise, home health care, and household services. In only two to three years, the Village's new president, J. Atwood Ives of West Cedar Street, expected membership to grow to approximately three hundred. Since this is a nonprofit organization, said Ives, any future profit should be shared with members. To ensure that the experiment serves all income groups, the Board of Directors of Beacon Hill Village plans to create an endowment drive with a special focus on assisting those in need.

The idea of such a "virtual retirement community" grew out of a grassroots brainstorming that began in the late 1990s, when friends and neighbors sought models for growing old together gracefully on the Hill. Initial discussions led to a series of focus-group studies and surveys among thirteen hundred residents over the age of sixty. The project was assisted by the Harvard Business School's Community Action Program and by the Rogerson Communities (the former Rogerson House), which manages both Beacon House and Peter Faneuil House on the Hill. Out of these efforts emerged a distinctive model launched in 2002—the first of its kind in the United States.

With the creation of Beacon Hill Village at the turn of the new millennium, the ancient Hill and its people have traversed a full historical circle. Nearly four centuries before, its community began as a New World village with Old World ties, growing immensely over the centuries in size, diversity, and complexity. Today, while it has gained a reputation for being one of the best-preserved historic districts in the nation, Beacon Hill is still charged with energy for renewal. The introduction of the Beacon Hill Village experiment by Beacon Hillers, for Beacon Hillers, symbolizes the vitality of this timeless community.

EPILOGUE

Myths of a culture can help all to remember the past and interpret the meaning of that past for the present. But there are also "myths in the making"—the way people in the present examine their own reality, create their own stories, and in the process envision where they are going. When it comes to such forward-looking mythmaking, Beacon Hill has certainly witnessed more than its share over the centuries. In fact, its history might be seen as a process of reinventing its own myth.

The earliest "myth" of the Hill, at least the earliest we know about, was created by the English settler William Blackstone. For him Shawmut represented a place where one could start afresh, greeting each day in a pristine forest, finding a respite from the onslaught of Old World events and a home surrounded by one's favorite books. The myth of Shawmut, as the Reverend Blackstone conceived of it, was short-lived. It gave way to the Puritans' vision of a "city upon a hill." In one sense, the Puritans shared and realized more fully Blackstone's dream of starting afresh, in their case breaking free from the autocracies of the Old World as well as its endless religious wars. But from another standpoint, the Puritan vision departed from Blackstone's love of the solitary; they envisioned a new community built on Puritan ideals and unburdened by Old World history.

By the late eighteenth and early nineteenth centuries, the Mount Vernon Proprietors reformulated the myth once again. They envisioned a large-scale residential neighborhood embracing within its borders a booming downtown business and political center, complemented with convenient accommodations. Enhancing the hill and filling the marshes, they transformed a wilderness into a real metropolis, and an elegant one at that. These nineteenth-century Proprietors had not lost sight of the myth of their forebears, however; they simply realized the metaphoric "city upon a hill" on a much grander scale, infusing it with a vigor adequate to the age of world trade and nation building.

As much as the Mount Vernon Proprietors appeared to be the masters of their lives and the creators of their own story, they could not have anticipated all the consequences of the urban village they helped to create. New historical forces required a new story with new chapters. As the Proprietors were laying foundations for their mansions on the South Slope, a slow but steady flow of African Americans and poor artisans was migrating up its neighboring North Slope. These residents built shacks and churches along the way, quietly undermining the aristocratic homogeneity assumed on the South Slope. Year after year an increasingly diverse mix of pedestrians rubbed elbows on Beacon Hill's narrow streets. Even the length of Pinckney Street could not entirely isolate rich from poor, white from black. Certainly not by conscious design, Beacon Hill was inheriting a heterogeneous population and a separate but shared history.

In the early twentieth century, the dynamic of Beacon Hill was made more complicated by problems of modern cities. The narrow, cobbled streets fell prey to automobiles and highway construction. Congestion, noise, pollution, and accidents threatened the gentility of neighborhood life. Even the endearing redbrick sidewalks became candidates for the endangered species list. With the rise of commercialism, and in the name of efficiency, there also came pressures to construct newer and higher structures. But the Hill's mythic identity was, by now, sufficiently grounded to avoid being overrun by such forces. In fact, shifting historical forces now merely set the stage for the community to express and prove its values more fully, playing out "the myth" in numerous civic fights and defending what Beacon Hillers believed in.

Out of spontaneous voluntarism emerged one of the oldest civic associations in America. From its birth in 1922, the Beacon Hill Association became an articulate voice for the community. Under the leadership of colorful and vigorous figures, the association lobbied politicians, pressed for new laws, launched public debates, and mobilized residents to fight for the interests of the Hill. Individuals such as Marian Nichols, John Codman, and Frank Bourne dedicated their lives to preserving the fragile fabric and antiquity of their neighborhood. If there has been a reinvention of the Beacon Hill myth in the modern period, it has come in the form of a community whose members saw that it was their duty to preserve the best legacies of the past and not to yield to a change until it meant a future that most of the members wanted.

Many Beacon Hillers proved themselves to be ahead of their time, especially in representing the needs of those less fortunate. As if to anticipate the coming Civil Rights movement of the 1960s, Margaret Welch, in 1945, fought for a civic association that would truly welcome as neighbors "the Jews and the Irish and the colored people." In the same year, the coalition of area churches, with the help of Beacon Hillers, foreshadowed a time of more sympathetic understanding of Asians by turning Number 6 Walnut Street into a relocation center for Japanese Americans. Dr. Koumans and the Reverend Scovel risked public aversion when they opened up the Parish House of King's Chapel to treat sick and troubled hippies. In the decades to come, residents and association members continued their efforts to keep low-income housing in the neighborhood.

For a relative newcomer to the neighborhood, the most impressive aspect of the prevailing Beacon Hill myth is the way the community has learned to face emotionally charged issues by keeping open the channels of dialogue and frank debate. The modern myth has been powerfully shaped by affirming and incorporating more fully the diverse voices of the neighborhood. It is certainly this openness that has afforded me, a new settler from China, the privilege of encountering firsthand the written and oral traditions of this grand old neighborhood.

The residents of the Hill have embraced the twenty-first century. They continue to make sense of new forces of modern life and what those forces might mean for the future. Instead of struggling over issues of building heights, they now lobby to regulate the effects of cellular antennae and individually owned satellite dishes on the skyline. To respond to growing social needs, Hill House has purchased the old Mount Vernon Street Fire House to expand its activities and services. With more young people moving to the Hill, a Young Friends and Neighbors Committee has been formed, creating more cultural and social events for this age group. As the baby boomers have aged, a new social experiment also has been launched to create a virtual retirement community on the Hill. Meanwhile, to preserve greenery around the Hill, representatives from the Hill have joined with the Neighborhood Association of the Back Bay to increase maintenance and care of parkland and memorials, hoping to protect and enhance the Esplanade as a treasured riverside park for all.

As new issues have been raised and new causes have been articulated, the underlying historic stage of Beacon Hill remains the same. The redbrick sidewalks, the gas lamps, the elegant Bulfinch architecture, the steady stream of tourists—all serve as daily reminders of the rich historical texture that time has woven into this storied place. This heritage reinforces pride and commitment, as it sets the stage for each reinvention of the neighborhood's colorful life. This, to me, is the enduring myth of Beacon Hill.

NOTES

CHAPTER ONE: A NEW VISION FOR AN OLD HILL, 1630–1900

1. John Winthrop, "A Model of Christian Charity," in *The Journal of John Winthrop, 1630–1649*, ed. Richard S. Dunn and Laetitia Yeandle (Cambridge: The Belknap Press of Harvard University Press, 1996), 10.

2. Barrett B. Rutman, *Winthrop's Boston* (Chapel Hill: University of North Carolina Press, 1965), 40.

3. Ibid., 75.

4. The State House Bulfinch designed later became Hartford City Hall.

5. Within a few years of the launching of the syndicate, however, Bulfinch sold his shares to Benjamin Joy. Woodword and Scollay sold theirs to Hepzibah Swan and the other remaining Proprietors.

6. Harrison Gray Otis also served as Speaker of the Massachusetts House of Representatives for two terms, as president of the State Senate for four terms, and as a U.S. senator.

7. The house was eventually relocated in 1925, some forty feet back from its original location, so that Cambridge Street could be widened. It has stood the test of time, like its two sibling houses, and is now the home of the Society for the Preservation of New England Antiquities.

8. He refused to allow his wife to bail him out since he believed the charges unjust, but he did allow Hepzibah to send him an annual allowance that made prison life more bearable.

9. Allen Chamberlain, *Beacon Hill: Its Ancient Pastures and Early Mansions* (Boston and New York: Houghton Mifflin, 1925), 61–69. The forty acres of land that today's South Slope comprises was purchased by the Mount Vernon Proprietors primarily from Copley, James Allen, and heirs of Enoch Brown.

10. Chestnut and Walnut Streets, for instance, were laid out in 1799, and Pinckney Street in 1802.

11. Beacon Hill has witnessed many such neighbor-driven actions in the two hundred years since the Proprietors and the State House construction first attracted public interest to the area.

12. Chamberlain, *Beacon Hill*, 80.

13. Jonathan Mason's house no longer exists.

14. Josephine Samson, *Celebrities of Louisburg Square* (Greenfield, Mass.: n.p., 1924), 5.

15. Chiang Yee, *The Silent Traveler in Boston* (New York: W. W. Norton, 1959), 29.

16. Oliver Wendell Homes, Sr., *Elsie Venner* (Boston: Ticknor and Fields, 1861).

17. Oliver Wendell Holmes, Sr., observed that Beacon Hill "holds the sifted few," referring to a comment by William Stoughton, a *Mayflower* passenger: "God sifted a whole nation that he might send choice seed into the wilderness."

18. Cleveland Amory, *The Proper Bostonians* (New York: E. P. Dutton, 1947), 48.

19. Dexter Smith, *Cyclopedia of Boston and Vicinity* (Boston: Cashin & Smith, 1886), 105.

20. Samuel Eliot Morison, *One Boy's Boston, 1887–1901* (Cambridge: Houghton Mifflin, 1962), 24.

21. *Bibliographic Sketch of the Colonial Laws of Massachusetts, 1630–1686* (Boston: Rockwell & Churchill, 1890), 53.

22. "Originally and naturally, there is no such thing as slavery. Joseph was rightfully no more a slave to his Brethren, than they were to him, and they had no more Authority to sell him, than they had to slay him." Samuel Sewall, *The Selling of Joseph* (1700; reprint, Northampton, Mass.: Gehenna Press, 1969), 8.

23. "Quock Walker Case," *Proceedings of the Massachusetts Historical Society*, 2d ser., 13 (April 1874): 294.

24. Nathan Appleton, *Letter to the Hon. W. C. Rives of Virginia, on Slavery and the Union* (Boston: J. H. Eastburn's Press, 1860), 17.

25. William Lloyd Garrison, "Preamble to the Constitution of the New England Anti-Slavery Society," in Robert C. Hayden, *The African Meeting House in Boston: A Celebration of History* (Boston: Companion Press, 1987), 23.

26. *The Liberator*, July 10, 1857.

27. Hayden, *The African Meeting House in Boston*, 35.

28. A. McVoy McIntyre, *Beacon Hill: A Walking Tour* (Boston: Little, Brown, 1975), 88.

29. "Ann Farquhar, Her Boston Experience," in *Fictional Rambles in and about Boston*, by Francis Weston Carruth (New York: McClure, Phillips, 1903), 47.

30. Ralph Adams Cram, *My Life in Architecture* (Boston: Little, Brown, 1936), 21.

31. Ibid., 220.

CHAPTER TWO: BEACON HILL RENAISSANCE, 1900–1930

1. Transcript of interview of John Codman by Stanley Smith, August 3, 1982, Historic Boston Collection, 30.

2. This is the land between Charles Street and the Charles River.

3. John Codman, in a private paper, wrote, "These promoters and their architects were friends of Mssrs. Codman and Street, and were heartily in accord with their vision of what the rehabilitation of the area should be."

4. *Boston Transcript*, August 21, 1926.

5. Ibid., April 12, 1930.

6. *Boston Sunday Advertiser*, January 23, 1921.

7. She went to Mrs. Quincy Shaw's School in Boston, which, recalled Marian's youngest sister, Margaret Shurcliff, "was a unique, and for those days, progressive school, backed by Mrs. Quincy Shaw

from idealistic rather than profit motives." Margaret Shurcliff, *Lively Days* (Taipei: Literature House, 1965), 7. There, young Marian was exposed to Mrs. Shaw's love for the concrete and the empirical in education.

8. Nichols graduated from Radcliffe a year later, *magna cum laude*.

9. Marian C. Nichols, Notes, Schlesinger Library, Radcliffe College, Cambridge, Massachusetts.

10. On the occasion of Marian Nichols's commencement, Professor Francis Cabot Lowell said that Radcliffe "has all along asserted to Harvard the right of women to higher education." In the lives of women like Marian Nichols, education had enhanced both their responsibility to society at large and their personal rights as women.

11. The Progressives also tried to give the people more direct control over the government by enabling voters to short-circuit the legislature and vote on measures at general elections. For three decades the Progressives made great strides in their fight for civil betterment, but, with the coming of World War I, the movement gave way to other concerns and many of the Progressives' accomplishments were all but forgotten.

12. From 1903 until her death sixty years later, she served as secretary of the Women's Auxiliary of the Massachusetts Civil Service Reform Association. In 1915 she became the first woman member of the Council of the National Civil Service Reform League, after being an examiner of the U.S. Civil Service Commission. Between 1922 and 1939 she was secretary of the Beacon Hill Association. She was also president of the Women's Industrial, Civil, and Suffrage League, and chair of the Legislative Committee of the Suffrage Association of Boston. The list of commitments and contributions goes on and on.

13. *Boston Herald*, May 2, 1963.

14. Marian C. Nichols ran for state representative as an independent from the Beacon Hill district. She won 775 votes, losing to the Republican candidates, James Hunnewell, who won 6,831 votes, and Lee Shattuck, who had 5,998 votes.

15. *Boston Herald*, May 2, 1963.

16. Nichols, Notes.

17. *Boston Herald*, May 2, 1963.

18. *HBI Report*, newsletter of the organization Historic Boston, Summer 1989.

19. Ibid.

20. Stanley Smith, comments made at the time of John Codman's funeral, March 29, 1989. Historic Boston Collection, 4.

21. The first meeting of the association, on December 4, 1922, served to formalize the organization and announce its creation to the public. It was not until the second meeting, in April 1923, that the top leadership of the association was finally put in place. Grace Minns abruptly resigned from her position in February and forever disappeared from the scene. The Executive Committee subsequently convened the same month and voted to ask Arthur D. Hill to serve as president and Mrs. Ralph Hornblower to be the vice president (her candidacy was unsuccessful). Arthur Hill accepted the presidency and recommended March C. Bennett as his vice president. They also voted to en-

large the Board of Directors from three to seven members, bringing in two new men, Felix Frankfurter, a Harvard law professor and future judge of the U.S. Supreme Court, and Bernard J. Rothwell, a former president of the Boston Chamber of Commerce. Also added to the board were two women: Mrs. Allen Chamberlain, whose husband authored the classic book *Beacon Hill*, and Mrs. Ralph Hornblower, the former candidate for the vice presidency of the association.

22. Helen Howe, *The Gentle Americans* (New York: Harper & Row, 1965), 128, 131.

23. Arthur Hill, quoted in "Barristers in Boston (III)," *Boston Globe*, December 16, 1964.

24. Howe, *The Gentle Americans*, 131.

25. The recommendations included restricting Beacon Hill to residential use free from business except on Charles Street; restricting Charles Street to local business use and confining it to the first floor of the buildings if possible; limiting the maximum height of buildings west of the State House to sixty-five feet or five stories; keeping additional business from being introduced within the area mentioned; and regulating the construction of future apartment houses on Beacon Hill.

26. *Boston Globe*, October 10, 1928.

27. *Boston Transcript*, April 12, 1930.

28. Anticipating opposition from members and neighbors, the zoning committee did not include lower Beacon Street between Charles Street and the Embankment in its proposal of 1928.

29. Frank Bourne to Marian Nichols, December 9, 1925, Beacon Hill Civic Association records (hereinafter cited as BHCAR).

30. Frank Bourne, Report to Beacon Hill Association, December 16, 1926, BHCAR.

31. The petition was from David H. Stone et al. of Cambridge.

32. Longfellow wrote, "I stood on the bridge at midnight, / as the clocks were striking the hour, / and the moon rose o'er the city, / behind the dark church tower." (He was referring to Charles Street Meeting House.) From *The Complete Poetical Works of Longfellow*, ed. Horace E. Scudder (Boston: Houghton Mifflin, 1922), 63.

33. A wood-framed church was built on the current site in 1737, but was subsequently razed by the British troops in 1775. Asher Benjamin rebuilt it in 1806.

34. *Boston Evening Transcript*, February 1, 1926.

35. *Boston Herald*, October 6, 1930.

36. Beacon Hill Association first annual meeting, Minutes, 1923, BHCAR.

37. Morison, *One Boy's Boston*, 22–25.

38. *Boston Transcript*, March 3, 1937.

39. It was not all bad news on the parking front. Beacon Hill residents pooled their resources and secured two parking garages on the Hill in 1925. The Charles Street Garage, at Number 144–160, built in 1919 on a 12,600-square foot parcel, held two hundred cars. Up for sale in 1925, the well-located garage attracted several interested parties, not all of whom wanted it to remain a garage. Twenty concerned neighbors, worried about the uncertain future of the property, formed a stock

company to purchase both the Charles Street Garage and the newly constructed garage on Cambridge Street. Entitled Charles Street Garage Company, the group wanted to operate the properties "under the control of residents vitally interested in the neighborhood." Together, the two garages held a total of five hundred cars. Even though the two garages could not solve all the parking problems, the Charles Street Garage Company helped keep the oldest garage on the Hill in the hands of its residents.

40. This was the title of Van Wyck Brooks's 1915 volume.

41. Lucius Beebe, *Boston and the Boston Legend* (New York: D. Appleton-Century, 1935), 303–304.

42. Ibid., 306.

43. Ibid., 309.

44. Ibid., 305.

45. Ibid., 311.

46. John R. Shultz, *Beacon Hill and the Carol Singers* (Boston: Wood, Clarke Press, 1923), 10, 11.

47. *Boston Transcript*, December 24, 1929.

48. Shultz, *Beacon Hill and the Carol Singers*, 11.

49. Cram, *My Life in Architecture*, 221

50. *Boston Herald*, December 25, 1931.

51. Shurcliff, *Lively Days*, 80.

52. *Beacon Hill News*, April 5, 1947.

53. *Boston Transcript*, December 18, 1934.

54. Ibid., January 26, 1935.

55. Ibid., December 28, 1936.

56. *Boston Herald*, December 23, 1937.

57. Ethel Bowen White, letter to the Editor, *Boston Transcript*, December 23, 1936.

CHAPTER THREE: WAR AND PEACE, 1940–1950

1. A letter from the Beacon Hill Association and a letter from the police station on Joy Street were sent to its members asking for volunteers to take air raid instruction classes. Captain Francis Tiernan's letter had asked the association to "secure suitable men for this vital first line of defense." Beacon Hill has never been short of volunteers for worthy causes. The letter asking to "secure suitable men," however, aroused some humorous responses from female residents of the Hill. "The notice said 'men,' but perhaps they are also using women," wrote Susan Herman. "In reply to your letter, this answer will surprise you," said another. "It is written to say that Miss Olive Seires of 46 Chestnut Street and I have just completed the Air Raid Warden's course at the Massachusetts Women's

Civilian Defense School. . . . If a real emergency arises in which women are needed as well as men, we would be glad to help in any way within our strength and natural limitation." It was signed August 2, 1941, by Hope Gray, BHCAR.

2. The dome of the State House was restored to its original gold color in June 1947.

3. Annual elections were held and some essential activities maintained.

4. Letter to John Codman, May 8, 1945, BHCAR.

5. Letter to John Codman, May 10, 1945, BHCAR.

6. Margaret Welch to Edward A. Taft, January 29, 1945, BHCAR.

7. Edward A. Taft to John Codman, January 31, 1945, BHCAR.

8. *Beacon Hill News*, March 1, 1947.

9. Ibid., March 8, 1947.

10. Ibid., October 24, 1946.

11. Ibid., March 1, 1947. The Community Church of Boston at Copley Square offered a series of courses on family relationships. Lecturers for the courses included faculty from Harvard University, Simmons College, the Family Society of Boston, and the National Council on Family Relations. The radio station WEEI also began a new weekly broadcast entitled "Marriage—for Better or—Divorce."

12. Ibid., April 19, 1947. The writer called himself "Epimenides." He indicated that he lived in an attic room on Charles Street.

13. Ibid., April 14, 1948. Allan Forbes, Jr., wrote, "It is with a sense of mixed horror and alarm that I read the Poetry Forum in the April 7th issue of the Beacon Hill News. In her discourse on war serving as an introduction to her father's poems, Miss Jackson speaks of 'the miracle of war.'"

14. Shurcliff, *Lively Days*, 113.

15. Ibid.

16. *Boston Traveler*, April 7, 1947.

17. *Boston Herald*, May 1, 1947.

18. Ibid.

19. *Boston Traveler*, April 7, 1947.

20. *Boston Post*, April 29, 1947.

21. *Boston Herald*, April 30, 1947.

22. Ibid.

23. Ibid.

24. *Boston Herald*, May 14, 1947.

25. Words and music by Francis W. Hatch, file in BHCAR.

26. *Christian Science Monitor*, March 2, 1949.

27. James Jackson Storrow, 1864–1926, a graduate of Harvard Law School, was a lawyer, a banker, the first president of the Boston Chamber of Commerce, and a member of the City Council. He had worked tirelessly to make the Charles River Basin "one of the noblest pieces of city planning in the world." Henry Greenleaf Pearson, *Son of New England: James Jackson Storrow* (Boston: Thomas Todd, 1932), 33–42.

28. *Christian Science Monitor*, March 3, 1949.

29. Ibid.

30. Their study concluded that the highway would not only fail to alleviate traffic congestion in Boston, but probably increase it. "If merely commercial interests should ever be given precedence over such high civic values as are represented by this beautiful waterfront park," wrote the Protective Association on March 22, 1949, "no warrant for such encroachment has been shown in this case." The Massachusetts Civic League also reached the same technical conclusion. In a letter to the *Boston Herald*, the league wrote, "unless and until an express highway down the embankment was connected with comparable and further facilities at the downtown end, it would in no way solve the traffic problem. In the morning it would result in an infinitely worse traffic snarl than now." *Boston Herald*, March 7, 1949.

31. Richard Wait, an attorney with the firm Choate, Hall & Stewart, filed a taxpayer's suit against the city, challenging the city's right to build a highway through the parkway, citing an 1875 statute that gave residents the right to protect parkland from encroachment. He argued that without consent to the city through an election, the land built as an esplanade in 1903 between Back Street and the walk at the river's edge could not be used legally as a public way. Assistant Attorney General William S. Kinney, representing the Metropolitan District Commission and the City of Boston, argued that the law cited by Wait did not apply because the parkland was acquired by the city by the right of eminent domain.

32. Rosemary Whiting, "Autobiography," 113. (This unpublished manuscript remains in its author's possession.)

33. Ibid., 209–212.

34. *Boston Traveler*, March 9, 1949.

35. *Christian Science Monitor*, April 9, 1949.

36. Whiting, "Autobiography," 212.

37. *Christian Science Monitor*, January 6, 1950.

38. During the first six months of 1950, Commissioner Callahan estimated that over thirty-three million dollars in public projects would be advertised for bids. Among them were several sections of Route 128 and a Springfield bypass of Route 20. Termed "Boston's traffic life-line," the proposed central artery would funnel traffic on an elevated highway from the Mystic River Bridge, with a connection to Storrow Drive, and through the North and West Ends to the Sumner Tunnel. It was expected to be completed in 1953.

39. The editor of the *Atlantic Monthly*, Edward A. Weeks, Jr., charged that the construction of a parking space beneath historic Boston Common "would irreparably damage its civic beauty." *Christian Science Monitor*, January 26, 1949.

40. The Boston Common Society called it "a desecration of the historic Common." *Christian Science Monitor*, July 13, 1950.

41. In 1908 George F. Parkman had bequeathed his residence on Beacon Street and five million dollars for Boston's public parks so that the Common "shall never be diverted from its present use as a public park."

42. In a letter to the governor, John Codman wrote: "Why would a private corporation be allowed to use public lands for what amounts to a public utility with no restrictions on rates to be charged, and with no city taxes on their improvements at a rental which could allow unrestricted profits?" This opened the way, said Codman, for the mayor to write his own terms with his own friends. Quoted in *Beacon Hill News*, February 4, 1948. Attorney John E. Hannigan shared Codman's sentiment and called the garage project "a barefaced steal." Richard Wait, a Beacon Hill resident who was active in the protest against Storrow Drive, also challenged the constitutionality of granting the garage tax-exempt status. The association commissioned the architectural firm Bourne, Connor, Nichols & Whiting to conduct a study of the feasibility of an underground garage. After a detailed analysis of the cost and engineering specifications, the firm, in its report to the Beacon Hill Association, concluded that a garage under the Common of proportions as planned would not be feasible.

43. Edward R. F. Sheehan, "Massachusetts: Rogues and Reformers in a State on Trial," *Saturday Evening Post*, June 5, 1965.

44. Sean M. Fisher and Carolyn Hughes, eds., *The Last Tenement: Confronting Community and Urban Renewal in Boston's West End* (Boston: Bostonian Society, 1992), 31.

45. The West End was originally called "New Field" or "New Boston" in colonial days. The first landowner of the West End was the Reverend James Allen. His pastureland stretched thirty-eight acres north and south of today's Cambridge Street.

46. *Christian Science Monitor*, February 1, 1956.

47. The first of the two federal housing acts was passed in 1949, allocating five hundred million dollars to assist cities with their urban development projects. The Federal Housing Act was passed in 1954. Its main objectives included the prevention of the spread of blight through strict housing standards, the rehabilitation of salvageable areas by replanning and other public improvement, and the clearance and redevelopment of nonsalvageable areas. The federal government hoped with the act to provide incentives to homeowners and private investors by extending credit and favorable mortgage terms to them. The Federal Housing Administration also provided mortgage insurance for residential rehabilitation and construction for families displaced from their homes as a result of government action. In the case of Boston, the federal government created a significant incentive for the city by providing two-thirds of the forty million dollars allocated for urban renewal.

48. *Christian Science Monitor*, February 1, 1956.

49. The chairman of the Build America Better Council of the National Association of Real Estate Boards claimed that labor demand for property renovation—in order to bring property up to a

required standard—"is sufficient to take up any employment lag resulting from a possible recession in new construction." The West End Project was also regarded by many initially as a solution to the dilemma posed by a deteriorated section close to the heart of Boston.

50. *Christian Science Monitor*, July 23, 1957.

51. Ibid., April 24, 1958. Both Piemonte and Lee foresaw the "human cost" of the project—the social and psychological consequences of displacing more than two thousand people from the only homes and neighborhood they knew.

52. Ibid.

53. Fisher and Hughes, *The Last Tenement*, 69. Federal red tape and controversies delayed the planned construction, while the BRA, in order to collect some tax revenue, leased the vacant land to private companies as parking lots.

54. Ibid., 83.

55. Ibid., 90.

56. *Christian Science Monitor*, December 19, 1958.

57. Charlestown, Jamaica Plain, and a few other neighborhoods were spared a similar fate as a result of the public outcry over the fate of the West End.

58. Two students from the Harvard Graduate School of Architecture, Carl J. Weinhardt, Jr., and Henry Milton, were recruited by the association to conduct a detailed survey of Beacon Hill.

59. According to Barbara B. Walker, then the publicity chairperson of the association.

60. *Pilot*, January 29, 1955.

61. *Christian Science Monitor*, January 31, 1955.

62. *Boston Daily Record*, January 10, 1955.

63. Ibid.

64. Rudolph Elie, "The Roving Eye," *Boston Herald*, January 14, 1955.

65. When the Beacon Hill Association was incorporated in January 1955, the name was changed to Beacon Hill Civic Association. Articles of Organization, January 26, 1955, BHCAR.

66. Gael Mahoney, letter to Beacon Hill residents, July 1955, file in BHCAR.

CHAPTER FOUR: REINVENTING BEACON HILL, 1960–2000

1. *Christian Science Monitor*, August 1, 1960.

2. Ibid., January 12, 1960.

3. Walter McQuade, "Boston: What Can a Sick City Do," *Fortune*, June 1964.

4. U.S. Bureau of the Census, *Census of Population and Housing, 1950–1960*.

5. *Christian Science Monitor*, August 1, 1960.

6. *Economist*, March 11, 1961.

7. McQuade, "Boston: What Can a Sick City Do," 6.

8. Gael Mahoney, speech at Beacon Hill Civic Association, February 7, 1957.

9. *Christian Science Monitor*, August 2, 1960.

10. Ibid., August 8, 1960.

11. Ibid., April 15, 1966.

12. Report of the Boston Historical Conservation Committee in the *Beacon Hill News*, June 1963.

13. Bowdoin Street lies parallel to Hancock Street on the other side of the State House; it runs between Beacon Street and Cambridge Street.

14. Representing the Park Service was Edwin Small, the regional director.

15. Owned by the New England College of Pharmacy until 1962.

16. *Boston Globe*, May 3, 1963.

17. *Boston Record American*, August 1, 1963.

18. Ibid.

19. *Boston Globe*, April 9, 1963.

20. Ibid., July 31, 1963.

21. Ibid., May 10, 1963.

22. *Boston Herald*, June 7, 1963.

23. *Christian Science Monitor*, October 22, 1965.

24. *Beacon Hill News*, February, 1968.

25. William Murray, letter to the Editor, *Boston Globe*, April 2, 1963.

26. Robert Reynolds, Editor-in-Chief, Editorials, *Suffolk Journal*, March 1967.

27. "I have a feeling for the old houses on Beacon Hill and the way they have been preserved," wrote Dorothy King, a resident of Temple Street, to the president of Suffolk University. "Looking just as they did a hundred or more years ago when our ancestors lived in them. With high rise and change all around us, the Hill remains a tiny memorial to the past." (Letter to Suffolk University, March 7, 1967.) Wrote Katherine Kane, a state representative: "This is not a run-down area of lodging houses; young families have been buying these homes and remodeling them in the best Boston traditions."

28. Members of the committee and other property owners also sent letters to the Board of Appeals opposing the granting of a variance to the university. They argued that allowing the school to expand into the residential neighborhood would not only damage but in time destroy the neighborhood and injure the city, much like what had happened to the Back Bay community.

29. "Once every decade a major dispute over zoning and building design seems to erupt on Beacon Hill," wrote the association. "Past generations have succeeded in using these disputes to reduce the maximum height of buildings along the edges of Beacon Hill, and in providing for a system of architectural review of the mass and appearance of proposed new buildings and renovations. A new and major crisis now faces Beacon Hill." Each generation should rise to its own emergencies, said the association, asking motivated members to finance the appeal to the higher court.

30. *Boston Globe*, October 17, 1967.

31. Ibid.

32. The committee sponsored the showing, at the Livingston Stebbins Center on Joy Street, of an antiwar film produced by the British Broadcasting Company entitled "Vietnam Journal." Among the local politicians they targeted was Congressman Thomas "Tip" O'Neil, whose realigned electoral district would include Beacon Hill. They petitioned him to hold open hearings on the war.

33. Interview with John Powers, a resident of Beacon Hill and an organizer of the Beacon Hill Support Group for Peace Action in Vietnam, August 31, 1999.

34. *Beacon Hill News*, February 1967.

35. Ibid., April 1967.

36. Ibid., November 1967.

37. Ibid., November 1969. Drugs became the magnet, said the *News*, "that makes Boston Common, Charles Street, and the Hill so attractive to hippies, junkies, and a familiar assortment of sightseers and hangers-on."

38. Ibid., September 1968.

39. Ibid.

40. This was created under the auspices of the Boston Metropolitan Commission. The task force was chaired by Robert Gordon of Pinckney Street.

41. Reverend William D. Hudson, "Has Beacon Hill Handled Its Hippie Problem Well," *Beacon Hill News*, February 1970.

42. The free clinic was open from 6 to 8 P.M. during the week and 3 to 5 P.M. on weekends.

43. *Boston Sunday Globe*, August 18, 1968.

44. *Beacon Hill News*, June 1969.

45. Ibid., February 1970.

46. U.S. *Census of Population and Housing, 1950–1970*.

47. *Beacon Hill News*, September 1970.

48. Senator Ames commented that the new center would "contribute a great deal to civic progress and betterment in Beacon Hill and surrounding areas." Mrs. John F. Norton of 6 Rollins Place, chairperson of the Association's Recreation Committee and later the first president of Hill House, presented an outline of what this centralized site could provide for neighborhood children of all ages.

49. Even though several other bids were received, with the highest bid at $36,650, the council voted unanimously in favor of the $1000 bid from the association, with an amendment restricting the use of the property as a community center only. Any breach of this provision would give the city the right to repossess the building. Responsibilities of the board included the maintenance of the center's physical condition, the establishment of policies and programs, and the liaison between the Beacon Hill Nursery School, the Beacon Hill Civic Association, and the Beacon Hill community.

50. Joseph W. Lund and Guido R. Perera, Co-Chairmen of 1966 Capital Fund Drive, "Letter to Residents of Beacon Hill," September 13, 1966.

51. "Articles of Organization," Hill House, May 10, 1966.

52. The play yard was transformed from a parking lot loading ramp.

53. The Reverends William Alberts and Frank McGuire and their volunteers supervised the program.

54. Jack Powers, chairman of the newly formed Education and Culture Committee of the Civic Association, suggested that a street fair would help bring the community together and restore pride in its main street. The idea caught on after some initial resistance. A street fair, many came to believe, could become a major neighborhood festival, creating a greater sense of community while serving as a bonanza for local merchants.

55. Many volunteers helped make the first street fair a success. Among them, Peggy Durkee provided an artistic hand with the publicity and signage, and Fifi Nessen organized the bake and book sales.

56. Some eighty more were added the following year. Even though fund-raising for the association was not an explicit goal, the first fair netted 132 dollars for the Civic Association; this was tripled the second year, and 3,800 dollars were recorded the fourth year.

56. New activities were added to the day, including the Museum of Science Traveling Animal Show sponsored by the Consumer Credit Union, a puppet show sponsored by Another Season Restaurant, and a pie-eating contest sponsored by the Suffolk Franklin Savings Bank. Among the Civic Association–sponsored events were a raffle with more than eighty-five prizes, a hot dog stand, a baked goods table, and a large children's game area. "You get a feeling of community here," commented the *Boston Globe*. In less than a decade, a modest neighborhood gathering announced by typed flyers taped to store windows, remarked the *Beacon Hill News*, had turned into a city extravaganza, with a volunteer committee of more than one hundred local residents (September 1982).

58. *Beacon Hill News*, September 1982.

59. Ibid., December 1978. There were about twenty condominium buildings on the Hill in 1976, according to the newspaper.

60. Ibid., October 1978. Beacon Hill had never, in its two hundred years, claimed Glynn, been a completely wealthy neighborhood. He, for one, enjoyed the hodgepodge of architectural styles and neighbors. If the West End had once been done in by bulldozers in the name of money and progress, this time "it is slower, and more insidious, and better dressed and mannered. But no less deadly."

61. Ibid., February 1978.

62. *Boston Ledger,* April 9, 1976.

63. *Beacon Hill News,* December 1978.

64. The committee first held extensive negotiations with the newly formed Public Facilities Department to reach an agreement on the sale price, settling for seventy-three thousand dollars. The total cost of renovation was estimated at one million dollars, 80 percent of which was construction cost.

65. The selection was Continental Wingate. According to the final arrangement, MHFA would provide a construction loan for one year. Upon completion of the building, a mortgage for a period of forty years would be given by the Government National Mortgage Association, from which the MHFA loan would be repaid. The apartment building was to be owned by the partnership of Bowdoin School Associates, which included a syndicate of investors with Wingate Development Corporation Trust as its general partner. The Beacon Hill Civic Association decided not to become a partner in the syndicate but retained its involvement in tenant selection.

66. The plan called for market-rate rents, with one-bedroom units priced at $384 a month, and two-bedrooms at $462. Twenty-six of the thirty-five apartments would be eligible for the rent subsidy program entitled Section Eight, administered by the Massachusetts Housing Finance Agency. Under this program, tenants would pay no more than 25 percent of their income for rent, and the program would subsidize the balance, including potential rent increases.

67. *Beacon Hill News,* February 1977. Ray Littlehale, the Civic Association's Bowdoin School Committee chairman, credited much of the success to such individuals as Stephen Oleskey, Bernard Borman, and Edward Lawrence.

68. Interview with John Bok, August 1999.

69. *Beacon Hill News,* September 1977.

70. *Boston Globe,* November 26, 1983

INDEX